RISING ABOVE

RISING ABOVE

How 11 Athletes Overcame Challenges in Their Youth to Become Stars

GREGORY ZUCKERMAN

with Elijah and Gabriel Zuckerman

PHILOMEL BOOKS

PHILOMEL BOOKS

an imprint of Penguin Random House LLC
375 Hudson Street
New York, NY 10014

Library of Congress Cataloging-in-Publication Data
Names: Zuckerman, Gregory, author. | Zuckerman, Elijah, author. |
Zuckerman, Gabriel, author.   Title: Rising above : how 11 athletes overcame
challenges in their youth to become stars / Gregory Zuckerman with Elijah
and Gabriel Zuckerman.   Description: New York, NY : Philomel Books, 2016.
Identifiers: LCCN 2015043688 | ISBN 9780399173820 (hardback)
Subjects: LCSH: Athletes—Biography—Juvenile literature. | Athletes—
Conduct of life—Juvenile literature. | Role models—Juvenile literature. |
Sports—Juvenile literature. | BISAC: JUVENILE NONFICTION / Biography
& Autobiography / Sports & Recreation. | JUVENILE NONFICTION / Social
Issues / Physical & Emotional Abuse (see also Social Issues / Sexual Abuse). |
JUVENILE NONFICTION / Sports & Recreation / General.
Classification: LCC GV697.A1 Z84 2016 | DDC 796.092/2—dc23
LC record available at http://lccn.loc.gov/2015043688

Printed in the United States of America.
ISBN 978-0-399-17382-0
7 9 10 8 6
Edited by Michael Green and Brian Geffen. Design by Semadar Megged.
Text set in 12.5-point Apollo MT Std.

To Shoshana, for all you do

TIM HOWARD

Tim Howard had a feeling he was about to play one of the toughest matches of his life.

It was July 2014, and Tim was in goal as the United States men's national soccer team faced Belgium in a key round of sixteen World Cup match. The stands in Salvador, Brazil, were packed with nearly fifty-seven thousand fans. Back in the US, twenty-two million viewers—more than the number who had watched the NBA finals or the World Series that year— were glued to their television sets, many of them skipping work to catch the game. Thousands more watched on a giant video screen at Chicago's Soldier Field.

In Washington, DC, President Barack Obama joined two hundred staff members in a historic building close to the White House, pulling hard for Tim and his teammates.

"I believe that we can win!" President Obama cheered.

The odds were stacked against the Americans. Belgium had finished first in its opening-round grouping, while the U.S. had tied for second in its own section. In its history against Belgium, the US team had four losses and just one win.

Before the match, Tim sat in his locker room, dressing the same way he did before every game. First, he put on his right shin guard, sock, and shoe. Then he did the same on his left side. Many players follow the same routine before each game, but with Tim it was more than habit or superstition. Tim *had* to follow the same pattern in much of what he did or he would become anxious and uncomfortable. He couldn't explain it. It was a compulsion, not a choice.

Tim began coughing and clearing his throat, over and over again. He couldn't seem to stop. His teammates, focused on the match, didn't pay much attention. They knew Tim was dealing with Tourette syndrome as well as obsessive-compulsive disorder. They were accustomed to his unusual behavior.

Walking down the stairs toward the soccer pitch with the rest of the American team, Tim was deep in thought, preparing himself for the big game. He ran onto the field and bolted toward his goal, nervous and excited, as the crowd roared.

"It was like I was floating on air," Tim says.

Suddenly, Tim looked up—he was surrounded by red uniforms, not the familiar white shirts of his American teammates. Instantly, Tim realized he had made an embarrassing mistake, even before the game had begun—he had taken a left toward Belgium's goal, not a right to his own.

Sheepishly, Tim turned around and sprinted toward the American side, hoping no one in the huge stadium had noticed.

"I was so tuned in, praying, thinking of my kids, that I looked up and saw I went to the wrong goal," Tim remembers.

After rejoining his teammates, Tim approached the referee, asking if he could hold the game ball. Tim turned it over, feeling the curve against his gloves. Back in goal, Tim bent and touched the grass. Then he felt the goal. Finally, Tim made the sign of a cross and said a short prayer for his children.

He followed the same ritual before each game, a result of his compulsive behavior. There was something about touching his surroundings that calmed Tim and gave him a sense of control he desperately sought.

"It's my security blanket when chaos is all around," Tim says. "I find shelter in my routine."

It didn't take long for Tim to come under heavy fire. Just forty-three seconds after kickoff, Belgium's Divock Origi bolted past the American defense, reaching the box with a surprising burst of speed. Tim moved to his left, squaring off against the young forward as Origi fired a cannon of a shot at the goal. Tim knocked it away cleanly, a big early save. The Americans breathed a sigh of relief, as did their fans.

"I got it with my right shin," Tim says.

Belgium put more shots on goal in the first half, but Tim continued to fend them off, one impressive save after another. Yet the Americans failed to put any goals on the board, either, and the first half ended in a scoreless tie.

The Americans weren't mustering much offense and pressure grew. But at least they remained neck and neck with the heavily favored Belgians.

"We held our own," Tim says.

Just ten minutes into second half play, something extraordinary happened to Tim and his teammates. Belgium's strikers began launching shots at Tim from all angles and speeds, an offensive assault that felt like it wouldn't end.

Dries Mertens headed a ball high on goal that Tim only managed to stop with an acrobatic leap. Origi took another thunderous shot that Tim barely nicked away. Kevin Mirallas seemed to have an easy goal when he streaked into the box untouched, firing a shot with his powerful left foot only to be thwarted by Tim's last-minute kick save.

"I barely got my left foot on it," Tim says. "Every time I looked up, there was a shot."

A buzz grew in the stands, among viewers watching at home, and on social media about the remarkable show Tim was putting on. They knew they were seeing something truly special. When regulation ended, the match still was scoreless. Somehow, Tim was single-handedly keeping the Americans in the game.

In extra time, Tim made five improbable saves, bailing the Americans out over and over again. Then Belgian star striker Romelu Lukaku entered the game, like a man on a mission. Lukaku stole the ball from an American defender and burst down the right wing, spotting Belgian midfielder Kevin De Bruyne running toward the middle of the penalty area. Tim slid to stop the shot, but De Bruyne spotted a crack between Tim and a defender and his shot found the net. A few minutes later, a wide-open Lukaku fired a ball past Tim.

Suddenly, the US was down two goals.

The Americans mounted a furious comeback, and teenage sub Julian Green scored on a gorgeous volley to bring the Americans within a goal of tying the game.

But it wasn't enough. The US team failed to score another goal and, in heartbreaking fashion, lost 2–1.

After the match, American fans were disappointed. But a funny thing happened. In spite of the loss, all anyone could talk about was how hard the team had competed and how remarkable Tim had played. His sixteen saves were the most in any World Cup in fifty years. Tim was named Man of the Match, an unusual honor for a losing team.

All over the Internet, people were in awe of Tim's performance. Some fans turned to humor to express their amazement.

A popular tweet that day read: "If Obama appointed Tim Howard to Secretary of Defense tomorrow I'd be cool with that."

Another one declared: "Tim Howard could have saved my parents' marriage."

In the locker room, Tim felt mixed emotions. His team had suffered a crushing loss. But Tim had played the game of his life. He had become a modern-day American hero.

It took a while after the game for it all to sink in, Tim says.

"I was emotionally and physically exhausted," he recalls.

Trying to come to grips with the events of the day, Tim sat back and took a moment to think about how far he had come in his career and life.

At an early age, Tim realized he was different from his classmates. Tim lived in a cramped one-bedroom apartment in New Brunswick, New Jersey, with his older brother, Chris, and mother, Esther. When he visited friends in wealthier neighborhoods, Tim was amazed to see high ceilings, lush carpets, and other comforts he had no exposure to at home.

Tim's father, a truck driver, moved out when the boy was just a toddler, and Tim's mother tried her best to make ends meet. Esther, who was of Hungarian descent, was a teacher who worked long hours, driving over sixty minutes to and from work. To save money, Esther clipped coupons, shopped at a flea market, and kept the heat so low the family often woke up shivering on bitter winter mornings.

At school, Tim stood out for other reasons.

"Why does your skin have that dark color?" a white classmate once asked.

Tim, whose mother was white, wasn't sure how to respond; he hadn't thought about his skin color before. Like many kids, Tim hadn't noticed his difference until someone pointed it out.

"My family went to Florida," he finally said, though it had been months since their trip. "I guess I still have a tan."

Tim wasn't like his classmates in other ways, as well. From birth, he was extremely sensitive to noise, touch, and light. Then, around the age of ten, Tim began touching items on his way through the house. First, it was the doorframe and the railing on the stairs. Then the light switch and the wall. Always in the same pattern.

Tim couldn't stop himself. If his brother gave him a jolt and the pattern was interrupted, Tim would have to go back to the beginning and touch the objects all over again before he could leave home. Tim understood what he was doing didn't make any sense, but he just couldn't stop.

"I *had* to touch these things and in exactly the right order," Tim recalls. "I knew it wasn't normal. I knew something was different."

When it began happening outside the house, Tim began to worry. He'd see a rock and just have to stop and pick it up. Tim usually forced himself to ignore the urges and keep walking, but a sense of panic would overtake him, his stomach churning. Finally, he'd give in and grab the rock, dropping it in his backpack, finding relief for the moment. Over time, his bag became filled with rocks, acorns, dirt, and flowers. Tim needed to handle them all to find some calm.

Tim started blinking forcefully and clearing his throat over and over. Other uncontrollable sounds and movements, or tics, soon began. Tim would jerk his face, shrug his shoulders, and roll his eyes.

He fought the tics, just like he did his urge to touch the various objects. The more he tried to ignore the urges, though, the more Tim felt stress building. He just couldn't resist if he wanted any relief.

Kids laughed or whispered about the unusual movements and sounds.

What's with your face?

Teachers snapped.

Stop clearing your throat. Sit still.

Tim's mother became concerned. Faced with the constant struggle to put food on their table, she had enough to worry about. Tim desperately wanted to ease her worries about his unusual movements and sounds.

But he couldn't stop. Sometimes he even had to touch people before speaking to them.

"I used all my energy to try to get my tics and twitches to stop. I did what I could," he says. "But it was a compulsion."

Soon, a doctor diagnosed Tim with obsessive-compulsive disorder, or OCD, a condition that affects over 2 percent of the population. OCD compels people to check or touch things repeatedly, perform routines over and over again, and have unwanted thoughts. The doctor also said Tim had Tourette syndrome, or TS, a neurological disorder marked by repetitive, involuntary movements and sounds.

"The doctor said my case was mild," Tim recalls. "It didn't feel mild to me."

School was a place full of anxiety for Tim, but he felt more at ease on the playing field. From the time he began playing organized sports at the age of six, Tim was taller and bigger than most of the other kids. He wasn't always the best player on the T-ball field or basketball court, but he usually was the fastest.

The soccer field didn't start off as much of a haven for Tim. After he joined a local peewee soccer team, the coach asked Tim to play goalie, noticing that he was tall and seemed fearless. Standing in goal seemed boring to Tim, though. And he hated giving up goals.

"I would get so frustrated I would cry when the ball went in," Tim told the *Wall Street Journal*. "My mom would have to come behind the goal and tell me to stay."

On the field, Tim began to notice he had a better handle on his unusual behaviors. When the action was on the other side of the field, Tim still was plagued by tics. But when the ball was on his side and opponents bore down on him, Tim felt totally in control. All the urges somehow disappeared.

"Sports were my sanctuary," Tim says. "Being outside, playing soccer or basketball, I wasn't focused on my tics, just on the opponent. I couldn't even tell you if I was dealing with tics. Sports were an escape."

The doctor who had diagnosed Tim with OCD and TS told his mother that some kids with similar disorders were really good at "hyperfocusing."

"With every challenge a kid faces, there's some flip side," the doctor had said.

Before long, Tim and his mother noticed the doctor was on to something. Most kids got bored and went inside after an hour or two of ball. But day after day, Tim would spend hours in his backyard, perfecting his soccer skills, step-overs, cutbacks, stop-and-gos. During soccer matches, Tim had a remarkable focus on the ball, his opponents, and the game. Nothing would distract him.

"I was completely and utterly focused," Tim recalls.

Excelling at soccer, basketball, and other sports gave Tim a burst of self-confidence.

"I was tall, strong, and could run by the [other] kids," Tim says. "I started having success and [receiving] praise from coaches and parents. My life was about positive reinforcement."

Tim competed in sports for another important reason: to make his mother happy. He knew she was overworked, overtired, and worried about Tim all day long. He couldn't afford to buy his mother anything, so he decided to play for her, hoping to provide her some joy.

On Mother's Day one year, Tim scored a big goal. He turned to face his mother on the side of the field, threw his arms in the air, and let out a shout: "Happy Mother's Day!"

To this day, Tim remembers the big smile she flashed in response.

One day when Tim was a teenager, his mother heard that Tim Mulqueen, the goalkeeping coach for the men's team of Rutgers University, a local soccer powerhouse, was holding a clinic for young players. She scraped together the twenty-five-dollar admission price, and Tim began counting down to the day of the clinic.

That day, Coach Mulch, as everyone called him, pushed Tim like no one had before. Coach Mulch fired ten powerful volleys at Tim, testing his skills and willingness to withstand the barrage.

"Move your feet together!" Coach Mulch yelled. "You've got to be ready."

After the session, Coach Mulch told Tim's mother to bring her son back for another session. When she confessed that she didn't have enough cash, Coach Mulch gave a surprising response.

"I don't care about the money," the coach said. He motioned her close, as if he wanted to share a secret. "Your son's got something, Mrs. Howard."

Tim trained with Coach Mulch week after week. He taught Tim how to think like a goalie, anticipate plays, and set up defenses. Some practices were so intense that kids were left vomiting on the field.

Early on, Mulch noticed Tim's tics and became concerned. The coach didn't want Tim teased, of course. But there was something else worrying him.

"He was so talented and so far ahead of the curve athletically I didn't want him to use it as a crutch," Coach Mulch says. "He's the first player I ever saw who could have played any sport, even Division I football, and chose soccer. I had to hold him to a higher standard."

Pretty quickly, Tim's teammates got used to his tics. That was Tim, unusual and special, no big deal, they seemed to have decided.

"He was such a good and talented kid that no one wanted to bring it up," Coach Mulch says. "Kids can be cruel when they see a kid with a disability, but it was never that way with Tim because he never acted like it was a disability."

Over time, Tim became even more serious about soccer. In 1995, when he was sixteen years old, Tim was chosen to play for the American youth national team in the Under-Seventeen World Championship in Ecuador. He and his teammates lost all three games, but they got a taste of high-pressure international competition.

Tim began missing school to train with the national

team, traveling to games around the globe. He soon caught the attention of professional scouts from Major League Soccer. When he was eighteen, Tim was offered a chance to play for the North Jersey Imperials, a junior club team associated with the New York/New Jersey MetroStars. Tim jumped at the chance, turning pro three months before he was scheduled to graduate high school.

In the middle of the 1998 season, MetroStars standout goalie Tony Meola was suspended for one game and Tim was picked to replace him as the team's starter. It wasn't clear how he'd handle the big opportunity. Before kickoff of his first Major League Soccer match, Tim couldn't stop clearing his throat, a sign of his growing nervousness. But he settled down when the match began, playing well from the outset. In the sixty-third minute, Wolde Harris, a top scorer, launched a rocket just yards from the net. Tim anticipated the shot, reaching out with his right hand and stopping it cold. It was clear to fans and coaches alike that Tim was something special.

By 2001, Tim had emerged as the MetroStars' starting goalie. Once, Tim had been embarrassed about his habits and tics. But Tim was growing more comfortable with himself. He got in touch with the team's publicity director, saying he had Tourette syndrome and was sick of hiding it. Tim was eager to talk about the condition with teammates and the public, hoping he might give encouragement to others dealing with similar challenges.

Newspapers and other media outlets around the country applauded Tim's courage. He began to work with kids with TS and OCD, urging them to be open about their own battles.

"It wasn't until I was around twenty that I could speak about it. I didn't have that self-confidence [before]," Tim says. "I was ashamed, but I didn't need to be. I wish I had known that."

In 2003, Tim got the call he had been waiting for. Manchester United, the most celebrated soccer club in the world, wanted him to join their team. Man U, as they're often called, already had a starter in Fabien Barthez, the goalkeeper for the 1998 World Cup Champions, France. But Tim was just twenty-three and he didn't mind backing up Barthez while learning from him and United's coaches.

The fan reaction to the signing wasn't what Tim had expected.

"United Want American with Brain Disorder" was the headline in the *Guardian*, a popular British newspaper.

"Manchester United Trying to Sign 'Disabled' Goalkeeper" is how the *Independent*, another well-known paper, covered the story.

Manchester United had more league titles than any other English club. Coached by legendary Sir Alex Ferguson, Man U was expected to win each and every match, no matter the opponent, much like the New York Yankees in baseball. Actually, they're more like the *old* Yankees, when owner George Steinbrenner tried to sign every top star and threatened to fire managers after a single losing streak. Manchester United stopped at nothing to put the best team together. At one time, the legendary David Beckham was their star midfielder. Soon after Tim joined, Manchester signed a young forward named Cristiano Ronaldo, who would go on to become a superstar winger.

One day during the 2003–2004 season, Ferguson told Tim he was starting a match against Arsenal, the team's heated rival. Tim knew the pressure and scrutiny would be intense. In a crucial first-half play, Arsenal's all-time leading goal scorer, Thierry Henry, prepared to take a free kick. Tim called for a three-man wall in front of him, to make sure Arsenal's attackers were guarded and Tim could see Henry's kick.

Henry's ball flew over the wall and found the goal's netting. Tim had let up a huge score early in his debut.

At halftime, Ferguson turned livid.

"That's idiotic! You needed four men on that wall," Ferguson bellowed.

He jabbed both index fingers at his forehead and screamed at Tim.

"You've got to think! I'll send you right back to the MLS! You're not in America anymore, son."

Tim didn't give up any more goals, and the game finished in a 1–1 tie. Over the course of the season, Tim improved and eventually became the club's starting goalie. Opposing fans continued to focus on his TS, singing insulting songs at matches, but Tim usually ignored the mockery.

"I heard the harshest things, but I never had an issue with it," he says. "After the game, some of the same fans calling me names were standing outside asking to take pictures with me."

Tim had come a long way from the time when he'd been too embarrassed to speak openly about his condition. That didn't mean that his days of being targeted for his OCD and TS were at an end. Nor did it mean his position on Man U was secure.

Just as Tim was adjusting to England and Manchester United, he made another huge gaffe. In a 2004 UEFA Champions League match against FC Porto, a ball flew past Manchester's line of defense. Tim knocked it away, but the ball rebounded to another Porto player, just yards from the goal, and he easily deposited it in the goal.

Tim had blown the match and he knew it. Tim also knew his coach had lost faith in him, as had some of his teammates. The coaching staff began asking if Tim's TS was affecting his play.

"I felt like I was back in school again. I had to hide my condition," Tim says.

Goalie is a position that often requires years of experience. Some keepers don't become truly great until they're at least thirty. Tim accepted his share of the blame, but he never got much tutelage at Manchester United.

"I felt isolated," Tim recalls. "It was a tough pill to swallow after my early success."

When he needed some help or encouragement, Tim often picked up his phone and called Coach Mulch back in the US.

"They never had a problem with my Tourette [syndrome] when I was playing well," he told his coach one day. "Now that I'm not playing well, they do."

"It doesn't mean you're a bad goalie just because you're going through a bad patch," Coach Mulch told him, trying to boost Tim's morale.

Tim's confidence was shot, and he began to dread matches. His performance suffered as a result. Eventually, Tim was benched, his career in jeopardy.

"It was a confusing time. It was hard to figure out what was next," he says.

Tim began to discuss a transfer with officials from Everton Football Club, hoping to escape Manchester United for a better situation. Everton wasn't as prestigious as United, but the team also played in England's first division. More important, Everton's coach, David Moyes, believed in Tim.

"What if I have a bad game?" Tim asked Moyes, worried he was going to lose his job again.

"Tim, you're young," Moyes told him. "I want you to learn."

Tim started off with several strong performances

and Everton's fans, known for their passion and enthusiasm, quickly embraced him.

"They reminded me, in many ways, of my own family: hardworking, determined, and hopeful," Tim wrote in his book, *The Keeper*.

As a boy, Tim wanted to do well on the soccer field to make his mother happy. At Everton, he wanted to make saves to make the raucous fans happy.

When Tim shut out powerhouse Liverpool—Everton's biggest victory over its crosstown rival in forty-two years—fans hugged and sang and screamed. Tim felt he'd truly found a home.

"That's when I knew I was going to make it in this league," he says. "I had a manager who believed in me, and it felt great."

Everton's players and coaches learned to accept all of Tim's unusual behavior. And he learned the team had its own unique rituals. One odd one: Everton players never close the bathroom stalls. Not even when they need to sit on the toilet. They see it as a funny way to build camaraderie. It took a while, but Tim eventually embraced that ritual just as Everton's players had accepted his own.

Today, Tim has played over four hundred matches for the team. In 2014, Everton extended his contract with the team until 2018, a sign of their confidence in Tim. He even made the record books in the 2011–2012 season when he booted the ball from his goal 101 yards into the opposing net, his first professional goal, becoming only the fourth goalkeeper in a Premier League match to score.

Some players would have wildly celebrated such a unique goal, but Tim felt sympathy for the opposing goalkeeper and refused to rejoice.

The key to Tim's growth as a player and a person: his ability to handle failure, a trait he's learned over many years. At Everton, he doesn't beat himself up after a big loss or gaffe, like he once did.

"You learn to compartmentalize, to move on [after defeat]," Tim told the *Wall Street Journal* in 2015.

Tim is considered by many to be the greatest soccer player America has ever produced. He's still Everton's starting keeper and fans around the world continue to congratulate him on his remarkable 2014 World Cup performance.

Tim urges kids to be comfortable with themselves, no matter how different they are.

"As a teenager, I tried to hide my tics and worried what people would think," he says. "But TS is just another detail in my life; it's part of me and part of why I'm successful. . . . I wouldn't change anything."

Coach Mulch adds: "A disease doesn't have to define you, you can still achieve greatness. We can learn from Tim that the way to deal with adversity is to meet it head on and not be ashamed."

Tim will be thirty-nine years old when the next World Cup takes place in 2018 in Russia. Many analysts consider him a long shot to start in goal for the American team; at that age, he may not have the same skills he did during his record-breaking performance in 2014.

Tim says not to count him out, though, vowing to meet the next challenge in his life.

"I'm going to push and claw and do my best to get on the team," he vows.

Once he became comfortable with himself, Tim was able to defy expectations and ignore skeptics. It's likely he'll continue to do so.

DWYANE WADE

Dwyane Wade felt a gun at the back of his head. He was just six years old and didn't know what to do.

Dwyane was watching cartoons one afternoon in 1988 when three police officers burst into his home on Chicago's South Side.

"Don't say anything. You walk and take me to where your mom is," a policeman demanded. Another officer, holding a silver gun to Dwyane's head, whispered in his ear, *"Now."*

Dwyane's mother was a serious addict who both sold and used drugs in her home. She even let others deal drugs from the apartment. The police were searching for her after receiving a complaint from a neighbor, as they tried to clamp down on a drug epidemic gripping the poor neighborhood.

Dwyane's heart was pounding. His body shook. He knew his mother was in the bathroom using drugs, and he didn't want her to be dragged off to jail. Dwyane walked toward the bathroom as slowly as he could, praying his mother would hear the commotion and quickly flush the drugs down the toilet, removing the evidence.

When Dwyane's mother finally opened the bathroom door, there were no drugs to be found; she had somehow disposed of the illegal substances. Dwyane felt relief. But as they searched the apartment, the officers discovered measuring scales used for drug dealing along with drug residue. Dwyane's mother was hauled away in a police car as he watched, fighting back tears.

Later that night, Dwyane's mother was released and back home, acting as if nothing had happened. Dwyane didn't know why the police had let her go, and he never asked for the full story. It was enough that she was home.

Troubles for Dwyane and his family were only beginning, however.

Dwyane's parents, Jolinda and Dwyane Wade Sr., had split up soon after their son was born. Almost immediately, Jolinda became consumed by drugs and alcohol. Most days, she wandered around her neighborhood or elsewhere in Chicago's rugged South Side, finding, using, and dealing drugs.

As a kid, Dwyane would wait on the front porch of his home into the night, sometimes staying up until 4:00 a.m., hoping his mother would return. When word spread that someone had died in the neighborhood, the Wade children, fearing the worst, prayed it wasn't their mother.

"There were many days that my mom left and we didn't know if she would come back," Dwyane told television personality Oprah Winfrey in 2012. "I woke hoping to see her."

At home, Dwyane's mother often was accompanied by a violent boyfriend who sometimes was the reason police raided the apartment. Dwyane didn't blame his mother, who could be loving and supportive, for her behavior. He loved her and just wanted her to be home with him. Above all else, though, he wanted her to somehow overcome her addiction.

"The only mother I knew at the time was a mother who was addicted to drugs," Dwyane says.

But Jolinda couldn't turn her life around and Dwyane couldn't help her. Heroin, cocaine, alcohol, and cigarettes were all Jolinda Wade seemed to think about.

She got high at home with her friends, leaving needles around the house, even with Dwyane and his three sisters nearby. Later, Dwyane would speculate that his mother relied on drugs—which she called "the madness"—to try to escape an overwhelming feeling of failure about her life and how it had spiraled downward.

Years later, Dwyane's mother described it this way: "I was embarrassed. I was miserable. I was really lonely."

Outside the home, it didn't get much easier for Dwyane. He tried to stay safe in a violent neighborhood full of abandoned buildings and intimidating gangs. The sound of gunfire was common, and Dwyane had no one he could turn to when he wanted to share his traumatic experiences.

"I've seen dead bodies in garbage cans and just walked by them," Dwyane later told ESPN. "It became common. . . . It was a rough childhood; my family was in the gang environment."

Sometimes, Dwyane would sit and listen as his grandmother, who lived a few floors away, prayed.

"Lawd, please help me with these children caught up in they trouble," she prayed.

Dwyane loved his grandmother and vowed to lead a different kind of life when he got older.

"I made a promise to myself never to do the things, whatever they were, that made my grandma sad and worried," Dwyane recalled in his book, *A Father First*. "That's what caused a switch to flip in my mind—seeing how much pain and stress 'the madness' had caused her."

Dwyane was happiest on Sundays in the summer when he went to church and then waited for his father to pick him up in his old, sky-blue Chevy. They would drive to a basketball court near his home where Dwyane's father played in a summer league against top-notch talent, while Dwyane sat nearby, watching and cheering proudly.

At home, Dwyane's older sister Tragil usually took care of him. Whenever their mother invited someone suspicious into the home, Tragil would take her siblings into a bedroom in the back and lock the door. There, they'd sit on their bed and ask God for help.

"If you take me and my sister out of this place and you save our mother, I will be someone worthy of your help," Dwyane recalls praying.

But Tragil was only four years older than Dwyane, and the family was having a tough time financially; there never was enough food to go around. When

Dwyane turned nine, Tragil knew she couldn't take care of him anymore. She took Dwyane to live with their father, who led a more stable life, hoping Dwyane could escape the violence at home.

In the first weeks away from home, Dwyane "felt lost, alone, and overwhelmed," he remembers. "Still, deep down, I understood that Tragil had saved my life."

Dwyane's father, a US Army veteran, was strict with Dwyane, and the boy thrived under the newfound discipline. Before, Dwyane's father wasn't always around because he didn't live in the neighborhood and was busy with his new family. But now that he had his son in the same household, he was determined to keep a close eye on Dwyane and teach him proper behavior.

Chores, homework, bedtime hours, and high expectations might have seemed a burden to many kids, but to Dwyane they were a lifesaver. Dwyane's father was a tough, talented athlete who encouraged him to pursue sports and dream of a better life. But sports were a reward. If Dwyane's grades were good enough, his father would give him and his stepbrothers extra coaching and drills on the basketball court.

Soon, the family moved about twenty miles away

from Chicago to Robbins, Illinois, allowing Dwyane to get farther away from the dangers and temptations of his old neighborhood. Dwyane's father built a basketball hoop in the driveway so his boys could play ball any time they wanted.

Being with his father gave Dwyane "the opportunity to be a kid," he recalls. "If I stayed in Chicago, I would have been the next in line to sell drugs."

Life at home was still chaotic. Dwyane missed his mother and visited her from time to time. But his mother couldn't steer clear of drugs. In 1994, when Dwyane was twelve, she was arrested on possession of crack cocaine with the intent to sell the drug.

Months later, she was serving time in prison, and Dwyane could only talk to her over a phone through a glass partition. Each time he came to visit, Dwyane had a confused look on his face, his mother recalls.

"I saw the look on his face. Like 'Why is my momma behind there? What's going on?' He didn't know what was going on. . . . He did not understand why I was behind that glass. And I was mad. I was so angry," Dwyane's mother said on the television show *The 700 Club* years later.

Back home, Dwyane headed to the basketball court

to get away from his day-to-day struggles. He idolized Michael Jordan, star of the nearby Chicago Bulls, and found basketball a distraction from the pain.

"The basketball court had become a place of escape and refuge, where no one would know what was going on in my life," Dwyane wrote in *A Father First*.

At fifteen, Dwyane was just five foot, six inches. He starred on the sophomore basketball team but didn't seem to have a future in the sport because of his limited height. Coaches were much more excited about the prospects of his older stepbrother Demetrius. He was such a good ballplayer that when Demetrius graduated high school, his basketball coach was despondent.

"I'll never have another player like Demetrius," Coach Jack Fitzgerald, with tears in his eyes, told Dwyane's father. "Never."

Dwyane's father told him not to worry too much.

"Dwyane could be as good," he said to Coach Fitzgerald. "Maybe better."

Coach Fitzgerald was surprised Dwyane's father had so much confidence in Dwyane. But the more Dwyane played, and the more drills his father made him do, the better he got. His father was a tough instructor, never content with Dwyane's play, always insisting he could do better.

"Dad was serious business, introducing us to fundamentals and drills," Dwyane says. "No glory moves whatsoever. . . . He never said a word to the effect that he saw anything special about me. . . . [It was] not his style, unfortunately."

It helped that Dwyane shot up four inches in the summer before his junior year. By the time he was a senior, Dwyane was six foot four and absolutely dominant on the court, averaging twenty-seven points and eleven rebounds a game, leading his team to a 24–5 record.

Though Dwyane began to thrive on the court, he couldn't achieve that same command in the classroom. Dwyane always liked school. Back in Chicago, he had enjoyed projects and other activities in his classes, appreciating a sense of structure he wasn't getting at home. But in his new school, Dwyane didn't always retain information well. He couldn't maintain proper focus on his studies. And he had tremendous test anxiety. Dwyane's grades were good, but his standardized test scores were disastrous. Many top colleges lost interest in recruiting him when they saw his awful early scores.

Dwyane took the ACT test a third time, hoping to score high enough results to be eligible to be recruited by a top college. He anxiously counted down to the day his score came back. When the day finally arrived, Dwyane received a huge blow. It was another poor result, so bad that Dwyane knew he'd be ineligible to play basketball for a Division I school.

Dwyane stuffed the envelope in his pocket, headed to the school bathroom, and cried like a baby. He had to splash cold water on his face to clear away any trace of tears before forcing himself to confront his friends, coaches, and family, telling them of his failure. Dwyane knew top schools would pass on him, and he wouldn't be able to play basketball until he showed he could handle college courses.

Luckily, one university was willing to give Dwyane a chance, albeit with a number of important conditions. Marquette University let him enroll and practice with the team as he attended class. Dwyane sat on the bench, acting like an assistant to Coach Tom Crean. But Dwyane wouldn't be able to play for the team unless he excelled academically.

Given the last-ditch opportunity, Dwyane didn't disappoint—by sophomore year, he had a grade point average of 3.0, proving he could excel in college, no matter the difficulty he'd had with the ACT. Finally, Dwyane was eligible to play for Marquette's basketball team.

Dwyane says much of his academic improvement stemmed from a newfound confidence he slowly was developing.

"I came to my own conclusion that if I could retain masses of basketball stats and information being thrown at me . . . there was no reason that I couldn't retain material for my academic classes or confront text anxiety," he says.

Once he was given the chance, Dwyane showed he could excel on the court as a shooting guard able to drive to the hoop against almost any defender. That year, he led Marquette in scoring and steals, and the team finished with its best record in nearly ten years. In the 2002–2003 season, Marquette won its first-ever Conference USA Championship and made its first Final Four appearance in twenty-five years.

In the Elite Eight NCAA Tournament game that secured Marquette's Final Four berth, Dwyane and the Golden Eagles faced the top-seeded Kentucky Wildcats. Kentucky was heavily favored going into the matchup, but the odds only served to fuel the fire burning in

Dwyane. In a spectacular performance, Dwyane recorded a triple-double, meaning the junior had double-digit stats in three different categories—twenty-nine points, eleven rebounds, and eleven steals. It was just the fourth triple-double in the history of the tournament and the first since Magic Johnson accomplished the feat at Michigan State in 1979.

Following his superb college career Dwyane was chosen fifth overall in the 2003 NBA Draft by the Miami Heat and never looked back. Continuing where he left off at Marquette, Dwyane was named an all-rookie selection in his first year on the Heat. In his second season, Dwyane was selected as a member of the Eastern Conference All-Star Team.

By the 2005–2006 season, Dwyane Wade had secured his place as one of the best guards in the entire league, demonstrating an impressive outside shot, defensive tenacity, and playmaking ability few guards could match. It also didn't hurt that Dwyane had been joined the season before by the legendary big man Shaquille O'Neal; with a duo as great as Shaq and Dwyane, the Heat quickly transformed into a championship contender.

That year, Miami made it to the NBA finals, where

they faced versatile forward Dirk Nowitzki and the Dallas Mavericks. Miami were the underdogs going into the series, and to no one's surprise, the Heat lost their first two games in Dallas.

Game 3 was suddenly a do-or-die matchup for Miami. Only a handful of teams in the history of sports have come back from a 0–3 deficit to win a best-of-seven championship series.

Going into the fourth quarter, the Heat looked doomed to defeat. With 6:29 left in the game, the Heat were down by thirteen points and it seemed as though their championship run was about to be cut short. But Dwyane refused to give up. In an incredible display, he scored fifteen of his forty-two points in the fourth quarter. The Heat went on a 22–7 run in those final minutes and upset the Mavericks.

That game proved a turning point for Dwyane and his teammates. Miami won the next three games to win the NBA title.

Gone were the days when the police would regularly come knocking at his door. Gone were the days when Dwyane thought he might never have the grades necessary to play ball at the college level and beyond. Dwyane had overcome the struggles of his past and become an NBA Champion. The cherry on top came when Dwyane was named the Most Valuable Player of the 2006 NBA finals.

Dwyane's incredible career was just getting started. After a string of all-star seasons, LeBron James and Chris Bosh joined forces with Dwyane in Miami. They proved a formidable squad. The Heat went on to win back-to-back championships in 2012 and 2013, cementing Dwyane's status as one of basketball's all-time greats.

The accolades and championships were great. But something that happened a few years earlier made Dwyane even prouder.

In 2008, Dwyane traveled back to Chicago to see his mother. After years of being urged by Dwyane and his siblings to get help kicking her drug habit, Jolinda finally had reached out for assistance. After a lot of hard work, she managed to get clean and turn her life around. While in state prison, she even had started a ministry to help others and spread the gospel.

On that spring day, Dwyane and his siblings watched as Pastor Jolinda Wade welcomed worshipers to her own church, in a building Dwyane had purchased for her.

"I'm so proud," Dwyane told the Associated Press before the service began.

That day, Dwyane cried once again because of his mother.

This time, they were tears of joy.

STEPHEN CURRY

There wasn't a single college willing to give Stephen Curry a chance. His dream of playing professional basketball seemed a long shot. A *really* long shot.

It was 2004, and Stephen was a high school sophomore. His father had played pro basketball and been a star. Steph grew up in North Carolina, close to some of the best college programs in the country, an ideal place to showcase his talent for top NCAA programs. And Steph had a passion for basketball, an accurate shot, and a hunger to make it to the NBA.

But no one took Stephen very seriously. He kept hearing how he was too tiny and skinny to play Division I basketball, the top collegiate level. The NBA seemed truly out of the question. It didn't help that Steph had a boyish look, making him appear even younger than his seventeen years. Big-name schools kept passing on Steph, figuring he couldn't contribute much to their basketball programs.

Those were the schools that actually knew Steph existed. Most of the best coaches hadn't even heard of him; they sure weren't going to recruit him or offer him a scholarship.

"I don't even remember seeing him [during his college recruitment process]," says Roy Williams, the legendary University of North Carolina coach. "I do know when I did see him I thought, 'Man, he is little.'"

Earlier in life, Steph seemed to have a lot going for him. Steph's father, Dell Curry, had been a first-round draft pick who'd played sixteen years in the NBA for five different teams. A six-foot-four shooting guard, Dell had retired from the NBA after a long career and remains the Charlotte Bobcats' all-time leading scorer and three-point shooter. Steph's mother, Sonya, had been both a basketball and volleyball state champion in high school and played varsity volleyball in college.

With such a rich athletic tradition in his family, Stephen played and enjoyed a lot of different sports growing up. But basketball was his first love.

"I was a competitive guy," Steph said in an interview on ESPN, "but something about basketball and doing what your dad did [made basketball] more of a draw."

Having a father in the NBA was a thrill, and Steph grew up admiring his dad and his skills on the court. His mother wouldn't let him go to Charlotte's games on school nights, though, worried he'd be exhausted the next day and unable to concentrate on his studies. So on weekends, Steph and his younger brother, Seth, attended as many of their father's games as they could. It was exciting seeing the best NBA players up close; it was even more fun watching their father compete against them. Steph and Seth sometimes even got to shoot with Charlotte players during pregame warm-ups.

In eighth grade, Steph decided to dedicate himself to basketball, determined to follow in his father's footsteps. He began practicing year-round, committing himself to doing "whatever it took, whatever was necessary, to play in college," he says.

By the time Steph was a sophomore in high school, however, he ran into an imposing roadblock: He was just too small. Steph stood five foot six and weighed in at a scrawny 125 pounds.

"On every team he ever played on, he was the smallest guy," his father says.

Steph was so frail that he had to begin his shooting motion well below his waist because he lacked the strength to raise the ball and shoot it from above his head. Steph's father knew there was no way his son could play college ball if he didn't change his approach. Shooting from below the waist makes it far too easy for a defender to swat the ball away. Dell knew college coaches never would recruit a player with that kind of shooting form.

One day, Dell came to Steph to deliver some unsolicited advice.

"If you want to play in college," Dell said, "you're going to have to bring [the ball] up and get it above your head."

Steph was happy with his shot and wasn't sure he needed to make such a dramatic adjustment. But he eventually understood he'd need to transform his game if he wanted to play with bigger and better players, as his father had advised.

Given his size, the NBA seemed completely out of the question for Steph, but he still wanted to play college ball, so he agreed to let his father tutor him. Steph took the summer off from his usual activities, even from playing pickup basketball games, to focus on reinventing his jump shot.

He didn't realize how difficult the process would be. All summer long, he and his father practiced and practiced on a hoop in their backyard. But Steph didn't seem to make much progress. Some nights ended in tears.

"It was tough for me to watch them in the backyard, late nights and a lot of hours during the day, working on the shot," Seth, Steph's younger brother, told ESPN. "They broke it down to the point where he couldn't even shoot at all. . . . He had to do rep after rep after rep to the point where he was able to master it."

"That was a tough summer for him," Dell agrees.

Steph worked with his father on changing his release point and moving the ball above his head in order to make his shot harder for rivals to block. Steph wasn't very muscular, so it was hard making the transition. But eventually the lessons kicked in and he began to master the above-the-head shot.

As they practiced, Dell and Steph developed a unique approach that made his shot both quick and accurate. When most players learn to shoot, they're taught to release the ball as they reach the highest point of their jump. But Steph was learning to shoot on the way up, when he wasn't very far off the ground. By shooting *as* he was jumping, rather than at the top of his jump like most people did, Steph could release the ball lightning fast, in as little as 0.3 seconds. That quick-shot technique would give him an advantage over defenders the rest of his life.

Shooting on the way up rather than at the top of his jump also enabled Steph's shot to take the form of a sharp arc, like a rainbow, making it much easier to swish through the net. Unlike everyone else, Steph's shots came in on a high angle, as if they were on a steep, downward slope to the opening of the basket. It was a distinctive approach he has maintained, more or less, throughout his playing career, according to the *Wall Street Journal.*

Back at school for his junior year, Steph's hard work began to pay off. That year, he averaged nearly twenty points a game. He also had a late growth spurt. By the time he graduated high school, Steph was six feet tall and weighed 160 pounds. He'd grown half a foot and gained thirty-five pounds in *two years*. Steph led his team to three conference titles and three play-off appearances and was named an all-state and all-conference player his senior year.

Steph seemed to be on the road to greatness and began envisioning himself playing for a nearby college power. "Growing up in Tar Heel country, you want to play for Duke, NC State, Carolina, Wake Forest," he says.

Yet none of those famed schools had any interest in Steph. Recruiters thought he was still too small and thin to excel at the collegiate level. Steph was developing a sweet stroke from the outside, but he just didn't seem like someone who could create his own shots, deal with bigger defenders in his face, and play in college, at least at the Division I level. Some overlooked high school players excel in Amateur Athletic Union leagues, gaining the attention of colleges through that route, but Steph wasn't an AAU star, either.

While most of the biggest schools had little interest in Steph, it made sense that his father's alma mater, Virginia Tech, might be willing to offer him a spot on their team. Dell had been one of the school's greatest basketball players, after all. And Virginia Tech doesn't usually go deep in NCAA tournaments, so the school often recruits high school players like Steph—capable and hardworking but with little chance of becoming NBA stars.

But even Virginia Tech, which plays in the competitive Atlantic Coast Conference, decided Steph didn't deserve a scholarship. The only way he could play on their team, the school's recruiters said, was if he "walked on," or tried out and outplayed someone else to earn a place on the team. They weren't going to guarantee a spot for Steph and wouldn't offer him a scholarship, no matter what his father had done at the school.

"I don't think he ever said it," Seth says. "But you could tell it hurt him."

Steph tried not to get discouraged, hoping a small school might give him a chance. That summer, Steph focused on refining his game and improving his shot, using the brush-offs as motivation.

The right college and coach will come, he told himself.

Steph needed someone to believe in him. He found that person in Bob McKillop, the coach of Davidson College, a tiny liberal arts school located twenty minutes north of Curry's home. Coach McKillop knew all the famous universities had passed on Steph, but he had a feeling they were making a big mistake.

Like other coaches and recruiters, Coach McKillop saw the deficiencies in Steph's game.

"He looked thin, frail, and not strong," Coach Mc-Killop says.

The coach knew something others didn't, though. His son had played Little League baseball with Steph as a ten-year-old, and Coach McKillop got to know Steph, watching him on the field, game after game. He continued to follow Steph closely in high school and knew Steph had special talent.

That's not what convinced him that Steph could be a star at Davidson, though.

"You could see the character, the poise, the work ethic, toughness, and resiliency," he says.

Coach McKillop got in touch with Steph and tried to convince him to enroll at Davidson, offering him a full scholarship. Sure, Davidson was tiny, with fewer than two thousand students and an average class of just fifteen. The college was best known for its academics and hadn't won an NCAA tournament game since 1969, let alone any major tournament. But at Davidson, Coach McKillop insisted, Steph could be a difference maker, a player with immediate impact. *Trust me and the program*, the coach told Steph. *Good things will happen*, he assured Steph.

Steph believed in himself and was confident he could enroll in a more famous school and make the basketball team as a walk-on. But even if he managed to make a big-time college team, Steph knew he likely wouldn't get much playing time. Maybe a few minutes here or there in mop-up duty at the end of a blowout. Playing a minor role on a team wasn't what Steph was hoping for, however.

Coach McKillop was the first college coach to make Steph feel he was wanted and that he could excel in big-time basketball. With that in mind, Steph signed on to go to school at Davidson.

"I could have walked on at an ACC school," Steph says. "But I wanted the opportunity to play."

In his very first collegiate game, Steph got the start at shooting guard, a sign of the confidence Coach Mc-Killop had in him.

It was a huge mistake.

The game was against favored Eastern Michigan on their campus, twenty minutes outside of Ann Arbor. Curry and his Davidson teammates fell behind early and trailed by sixteen points at halftime, an early destruc-tion. By halftime, Steph had *nine* turnovers. He would finish with a humiliating thirteen turnovers in total.

Steph seemed truly out of his league in Division I basketball, just like the college coaches had predicted. In one embarrassing play, Steph handled the ball in the backcourt, as defenders swarmed around him, and quickly lost his footing. Slipping and falling to the court awkwardly, Steph flung the ball to a teammate, only to see an opposing player step in and knock it away. The Eastern Michigan fans cheered wildly, celebrating the ugly mistake. Davidson fans cringed.

At halftime, even Steph's coach had second thoughts about him. "I'm rethinking whether he belongs in the starting lineup," Coach McKillop remembers contemplating.

In spite of his reservations, Coach McKillop decided to leave Steph in for the second half, hoping he might settle down. *Smart* move. Almost immediately, Steph and his team began to rally. Instead of acting discouraged or scared after the awful first half, Steph called for the ball, camping out on the three-point line, begging teammates to feed him the rock. Steph began knocking down threes, one after another, becoming more confident with each bucket. He quieted the hostile crowd and led Davidson to an improbable comeback victory.

It was an early sign of Steph's self-assurance and tenacity.

The next night, against an even more imposing University of Michigan team, Steph really went off. He scored thirty-two points, dished out four assists, and even snatched nine rebounds.

Steph finished his freshman year as the leading scorer in the Southern Conference, averaging 21.5 points per game, second in the nation among freshmen, just behind University of Texas forward Kevin Durant, a future NBA superstar. Steph also broke the freshman season record for three-point field goals.

One day that year, Coach McKillop spotted Steph's parents in the airport and walked over, making a prediction: "Your son will earn a lot of money playing this game one day."

Dell Curry was skeptical. A great college shooter is one thing. Making it at the pro level is a whole different ball game. Even though he'd had a late growth spurt, Steph was still short and slight, especially compared with guys in the NBA. Guarding big, muscular players in the pros seemed improbable. As far as Dell was concerned, Steph's chances of succeeding in the NBA, or even getting drafted by a team, weren't very strong; Coach McKillop's prediction seemed foolish.

"I'm thinking, 'Yeah, maybe [he'll have a chance to play] overseas,'" Dell Curry says.

But Steph kept growing, reaching six foot three inches by his sophomore year in college. And he continued to perfect his shot. On March 21, 2008, Steph and Davidson played in the NCAA Tournament. With his parents in the stands and a national audience glued to their television screens, Steph dropped an astounding forty points on Gonzaga University, shooting an astonishing eight for ten from three-point range, leading Davidson to its first NCAA Men's Basketball Tournament win since 1969. Two days later, Steph burned heavily favored Georgetown University, the nation's eighth-ranked team, for thirty points in another upset victory.

His parents watched from the stands, absolutely stunned. Steph was evolving from a good player into a great one before their eyes.

"Can you believe that?" Dell asked his wife.

They were so shocked they drove home from the game in silence, Steph's mother, Sonya, recalls.

During that year's tournament, Steph emerged as a household name around the country, becoming only the fourth player in history to average at least thirty points in his first four NCAA Tournament games and leading Davidson to the Elite Eight, where the team lost to the top-seeded and eventual champion Kansas Jayhawks.

"He changed from him being Dell's son to Dell being Steph's father," Seth says.

Steph's head-turning performance on a national

stage dramatically altered the way he was viewed in the basketball world and beyond. After the NCAA Tournament ended, his parents saw up close how much Steph's life and career had transformed in just a few days. At a Charlotte home game, they watched fans mob Steph, as if he was a rock star.

"That's how I knew things had changed," Sonya says.

After leading the nation with an average of almost twenty-nine points per game in his junior year, Steph declared himself eligible for the 2009 draft. He still had legions of doubters, though. At six foot three, Steph was above-average height for an NBA point guard. But he lacked muscle and it wasn't clear he could handle the physical toll of NBA games or defend athletic guards in the pros.

"I heard the same stuff [I'd always heard throughout my life]," he says. "I'm too small, not athletic enough, can't play defense, not strong enough."

On the outside, Steph acted confident he could handle the next level. But inside, Steph shared some of the same concerns others had about whether he could make it in the pros. Steph was still baby faced, frail, and thin. How was he going to defend tall, muscular, or super-quick guards like Dwyane Wade, Kobe Bryant, and Tony Parker?

"I was nervous," he told ESPN. "Obviously that transition is a big deal."

Steph already was becoming a fan favorite, thanks to his sweet shot and boyish looks. When he was picked seventh in the first round by the Golden State Warriors, fans in Madison Square Garden erupted. Some cheered; others were upset he didn't drop another spot so the hometown New York Knicks could grab him with the eighth pick. That year, Steph had a strong debut season, finishing with an average of 17.5 points, 4.5 rebounds, 5.9 assists, and 1.9 steals per game. He was unanimously selected as a member of the All-Rookie First Team and finished second in the NBA Rookie of the Year Award voting.

But his body began to become a liability, just as the experts had feared. In the 2011–2012 season, Steph missed forty-eight games, dealing with two ankle surgeries. Some wondered if his injury woes would become chronic and whether Steph would become another Grant Hill—a former NBA player with unlimited potential who saw his career cut short by ankle troubles.

"Every question I got was 'How are your ankles?'" Steph says.

Steph spent six months rehabilitating, turning to his family for comfort and support. He tried his best to tune out skeptics who doubted his long-term prospects.

"It was really tough," Dell recalls.

Many players get to the pros and are happy just to be in the NBA. But Steph's goal was to be a star, not just an ordinary player. Steph had averaged eighteen points a game and 5.9 assists during his first two years at Golden State—impressive numbers, but not good enough to make an All-Star Team. He was determined to prove the skeptics wrong and show he could become one of the NBA's best guards.

Steph already was a deadeyed shooter. His dribbling and ball-handling skills weren't nearly as impressive, though. In college, the flaws in his game hadn't mattered very much because he'd been a shooting guard until his junior year, which meant he'd often come off screens for open shots. He hadn't needed to pass or dribble very much while filling that role. His teammates' screens helped him get open looks at the basket. But now, as an NBA point guard, Steph didn't have a chance at becoming an elite player unless he somehow turned his dribbling and passing weaknesses into strengths.

During the NBA lockout in the summer of 2011, Steph decided to rework his game, just as he had with his father as a child. It took a lot of courage for Steph to admit he was good but not good enough.

Steph hired a trainer and began intensive daily workouts at a local gym near his hometown of Charlotte, North Carolina, working on a series of unique and challenging drills, each with the goal of improving a different facet of Steph's game. One drill, aimed at making Steph dribble with more force and confidence, involved dribbling two balls at the same time, one a normal basketball, the other a much heavier and less bouncy ball. By dribbling harder, Steph learned to move the ball more quickly from the floor to his hand, helping him navigate tight spaces on the court, moving in and out of traffic. The drill also made his hands faster and stronger.

Another drill involved tossing a tennis ball in the air, dribbling a basketball behind his back, and catching the tennis ball before it hit the floor. Steph's dribbling and passing skills were getting better, but he wasn't there yet.

His drills became more complicated and challenging. Steph performed a series of between-the-leg and behind-the-back dribbles with one hand while his other hand was occupied. Sometimes, Steph dribbled with one hand and waved a forty-pound rope in the other, for example. Later, Steph incorporated a drill in which he dribbled while wearing goggles that cut off vision in one eye, to improve his court vision and passing.

Over time, Steph's dribbling became as extraordinary as his shooting. Now that he could dribble through traffic and around defenders with ease, he knew he'd have more space for his outside shot because defenders would have to respect his dribbling ability. He also was sure his passing skills had improved dramatically. Steph couldn't wait for the season to begin so he could unveil his new all-around game.

In November 2012, Steph returned for his fourth NBA season. He was healthy, finally, still deadly from downtown and ready to unleash his revamped game featuring moves few had ever seen. Ankle-breaking crossovers. Quick changes of direction in super-tight spaces. Behind-the-back bounce moves. Steph's new skill set left defenders reeling. Just as he suspected, the moves created space for Steph to find open shots or to hit teammates with bull's-eye passes. In the 2012–2013 season, Steph averaged 22.9 points, 6.9 assists, and 4.0 rebounds per game; he even scored a career-high fifty-four points in a loss against the New York Knicks, going eighteen for twenty-eight from the field.

As his game improved, Steph felt he deserved to represent the Warriors in that year's NBA All-Star Game. Before a midseason matchup in Chicago, Steph waited in his hotel room for the Western Conference All-Star Team selections to be announced, sure his name would be called. The wait seemed to drag on forever. Finally, the roster was announced—to Steph's shock, he didn't make the cut.

Steph had been overlooked once again.

He sat in the room for several minutes, dejected. It was a disappointing moment he would remember for years.

Whenever he got down or experienced a rough game, Steph often returned to the Warriors' locker room to find a text message waiting for him from his old college coach. Usually it was some helpful advice, sometimes in language that only Steph could understand.

Sleep in the streets, Coach McKillop often would text, for example.

Steph knew what the cryptic message meant—his old coach was sharing a lesson from former NBA player and coach Kevin Loughery. When life's rough and you're missing your shots or dealing with other kinds of disappointments, the only way to respond is to practice your heart out, even if it takes all night, leaving you locked out of your home and forced to sleep in the streets.

Coach McKillop was telling Steph that the best response to a setback is to work even harder.

Steph got the message.

Gonna be sleeping in the streets tonight, Steph texted right back to Coach McKillop.

Instead of dwelling on the All-Star diss, Steph decided to continue working on his game. Later that season, Steph set the single-season record for three-pointers and led the Warriors to the play-offs, losing in the second round to the San Antonio Spurs.

During the 2013–2014 season, Steph was rewarded for his hard work. This time, when the All-Star Team rosters were announced, Steph's name was called. Not only did he make the team, but he was voted in as a starter.

The kid who many had thought had little to no

chance of making the NBA was officially a star, finishing the year with 24 points and 8.5 assists a game.

At the end of the 2014–2015 season, Steph was named the NBA's Most Valuable Player, adding to his resume as an elite player. To cap off his incredible season, Steph led the Warriors to victory in the NBA finals, defeating LeBron James and the Cleveland Cavaliers. Steph also had become one of the league's most popular players, with the second-highest-selling jersey—at that, at least, he could not defeat LeBron James, whose jersey held the top spot.

Steph was on his way to setting NBA records. By the end of the 2015 calendar year, no active or retired player who'd attempted more than two thousand three-pointers could match Steph's 44 percent shooting percentage. He also ranked fifth in free-throw percentage among qualified players, shooting 90 percent from the line.

"Curry three-pointers are like everyone else's dunks," the *Wall Street Journal* wrote that year. "Only his misses are surprising. To watch Stephen Curry play basketball is to witness a shooter unlike any the NBA has ever seen."

In the winter of 2015, Steph visited Madison Square

Garden, the mecca of the basketball world, for a show-down with the New York Knicks. He racked up twenty-two points with relative ease, hitting open men and putting on a dribbling clinic, flashing big smiles after nice plays and receiving the Garden's loudest cheers, a rarity for a visiting player.

In the locker room after the game, while icing his knees and dealing with scratches on both arms—souvenirs from aggressive defenders who had failed to slow him down—Steph took time to share his thoughts on his unlikely career. That night, he had heard wild cheering at the Garden, Steph acknowledged. But he said he couldn't forget the sting of the many insults and disappointments suffered years earlier, when he couldn't manage to grab the attention of college re-cruiters, heard skepticism about his pro prospects, and then couldn't crack the NBA All-Star Team.

"Two years ago, I was snubbed, and now I get acco-lades," he said. "It's crazy."

Asked what advice he had for young people having their own troubles gaining appreciation and attention, Steph urged patience.

"Find your niche and find ways to have fun on the court, hold yourself to a high standard," he said.

"If you have the right attitude, you'll eventually get noticed. . . . Nowadays, scouts will find you, wherever you are."

He shared other advice relevant for basketball and for life. Talent only takes you part of the way, he said. To be a success, much more is needed.

"If you dream big and work hard, you'll see results," Steph said with a smile. "It's the hard work that separates you."

JIM ABBOTT

Jim Abbott was getting nervous.

It was the summer of 1987, and Jim was on his way to Cuba with the rest of the USA Baseball team, a group of college students chosen to compete against the best amateur international clubs from around the world.

The Cuban team was amateur in name only. Many of its players were in their late twenties and thirties and had years of experience playing in semiprofessional leagues in Cuba. Cuban citizens weren't allowed to leave the country to play baseball, so none of the players on the team had ever played in the major leagues. Yet scouts said the lineup was packed with some of the most powerful hitters on the planet, players who easily could have been major-league stars.

The US team boasted its own share of talent. That

year, Jim, a left-handed pitcher, had been named the top amateur baseball player in the nation after leading the University of Michigan to the Big Ten Championship. His teammate Frank Thomas would go on to become a Hall of Fame first baseman for the Chicago White Sox. Tino Martinez would win four World Series rings as a slugging first baseman for the New York Yankees.

But the American team seemed overmatched. It was composed of college sophomores and juniors. And this wasn't just any old game—it was a historic matchup. An American team hadn't played a game on Cuban soil in twenty-five years. As they landed in Cuba for a five-game series in the baseball-crazy nation, Jim was nervous. Representing his country was a lot to ask of the young man.

"We were a bunch of college kids; it was a lot to carry," Jim says.

Jim always had issues with his confidence. Sometimes he felt he could throw his fastball so hard opponents didn't stand a chance. Other days, Jim wondered how he'd be able to get anyone out.

There was another reason Jim was apprehensive as he walked off the plane: He had been born without a right hand, and he dreaded those moments when people focused on his physical difference. Now he braced for a crush of Cuban fans.

Growing up, Jim did his best to deal with his difference. He laughed when others made jokes, cracked a few of his own, and hoped his talent on the mound would cause people to forget about his missing hand. That strategy usually worked. But meeting new people or playing in foreign locations always made Jim uncomfortable.

Now, as he grabbed his suitcase at the airport terminal, dozens of Cuban fans rushed over to photograph his right arm, shoved deep into his pocket. As the team tried to leave the airport, another throng of curious Cuban fans surrounded the bus, delaying their departure.

Here we go again, Jim thought.

Jim felt pangs of guilt knowing that he was inconveniencing his teammates and coaches.

"I felt like an outsider on my own team, apart from everyone," Jim recalls.

To make matters worse, the USA team dug a deep hole for themselves early in the series, losing the first two games. One more loss and the Cubans would walk away with an easy series victory, along with bragging rights over the country that had invented the sport.

Jim was slotted to be the starting pitcher of that pressure-filled third game.

As Jim took the mound, he could feel the tension mounting. A local paper had announced that a "one-handed pitcher" would start for the American team. Whole sections of the stadium stood and watched Jim take warm-up pitches. Peering into the stands, it seemed like the whole country was there, watching his every move. In Cuba, baseball is more than just a sport. To players and fans, games are closer to life-or-death grudge matches; everything is on the line.

As the buzz from the crowd grew, Cuba's leader, Fidel Castro, wearing military fatigues made of silk, emerged from the dugout to welcome the players. To Jim, Castro seemed even bigger and more intimidating than he did on television.

While throwing his warm-up tosses, Jim noticed a couple thousand fans standing. Some leaned over stadium railings, chanting Jim's name, heckling and pointing at him. Music blasted. Horns, bongos, and sirens added to the clamor and fed the intensity.

"I wanted to prove them wrong, that I wasn't just an oddity," he says.

Jim waited on the mound, ready for the game's first pitch. The Cuban leadoff batter, a cocky twenty-seven-year-old named Victor Mesa, sauntered to the plate. Mesa was a fleet center fielder, one of the best hitters the nation ever had produced. Flamboyant and super-fast, Mesa didn't just swipe bases, including home on a regular basis, he often did so while taunting opposing pitchers, sending the Cuban crowd into hysterics.

More than fifty thousand rowdy fans stood and screamed, waiting to see if the Cuban batters would take advantage of Jim's disability.

"Fans were going crazy," Jim recalls. "It made Yankee Stadium seem tame."

Jim focused in on Mesa. Mesa twirled his bat, trying to unnerve Jim. Cradling his glove on the end of his right forearm, like usual, Jim reached back with his left hand to fire the game's first pitch. As a fastball came in, letter high, Mesa shifted his hands quickly—he was trying to surprise Jim by laying down a bunt toward third base. He was forcing Jim to somehow field, pivot, and throw Mesa out, all with just one hand.

Jim bounded off the mound, lightning quick. He barehanded the ball with his left hand, turned, and fired to first as Mesa sprinted down the first-base line. Out by a half step!

The fans exploded, whistling and screaming. As Jim took it all in, he sensed they were getting on Mesa—and showing Jim their appreciation. He had won them over.

"The fans' attitude went from curiosity to respect," he says. "It was a cool moment."

The Cuban players learned Jim could field his position, despite his difference. No other Cuban players dared to bunt on Jim for the rest of the game, and he cruised to victory. The US ended up losing the series, but Jim had overcome one of the biggest challenges of his life.

It was a sign of things to come.

The doctor found Mike Abbott pacing the waiting room of the Flint, Michigan, hospital. It was an early fall day in 1967, and Mike had been waiting anxiously.

"You have a fine baby boy," the doctor began, "but . . ."

Mike's sister reached out to support her brother.

". . . he was born without one of his hands."

Mike was stunned. So was Jim's mother, Kathy, who was resting in a nearby delivery room. Having a baby at any age is overwhelming. But Mike and Kathy were just nineteen years old and they were being told their son had been born without a right hand.

Doctors called it a fluke, a birth defect with no explanation. For Mike and Kathy, it was a staggering blow. They tried their best to deal with the news. With love and support, Jim would do fine, they eventually decided. Maybe even better than fine.

For the first few years of his life, Jimmy seemed like any other boy, capable of doing pretty much everything other kids could do. His physical difference was hard to miss, though. Jimmy's right arm was small and weak, and it ended close to his wrist. By the age of five, doctors had concluded the boy should be fitted with a prosthetic arm and a mechanical hand to help him later in life.

Jim spent a month in a Michigan hospital as specialists fit him with an artificial arm and metal hook for a hand. It was a lonely experience. The hospital was about two hours away from home. Mike and Kathy were barely making ends meet and couldn't take time off from work, so they could visit their son only on weekends. Jim and the other kids in the hospital, some of whom were missing arms or legs, had nets covering their beds, a crude effort to ensure they didn't stray too far.

After he finally went home, Jim did his best to adjust to the prosthesis. At times, he even had fun with it. That summer, the six-year-old shocked guests at a family barbecue by using his metal hook to flip burning steaks on the hot grill. Other times, he amused himself by smashing bottles and breaking wooden planks.

But it didn't take long before little Jimmy began to loathe his bulky, hot, and uncomfortable artificial arm and hand. The worst part was the unwanted attention it drew when he began going to school.

One day a few years later, Jim walked up to a group of girls. Before he had a chance to speak, the girls turned and fled, shrieking with fear.

"Ugh!" one of the girls cried.

The girls didn't mean to crush Jim's feelings; they had never seen anyone who looked like he did. Jim stood in place, flushed with embarrassment.

"That was hard to handle because I couldn't do anything to address it," Jim recalls. "It happened a lot."

No one had given Mike and Kathy a playbook for these kinds of situations. They decided to shower

Jimmy with love and encouragement, telling him that he could do anything other kids could do. To them, he was like any other child. He just happened to be physically different.

"My parents were young, this was unexpected, and it was hard for them," Jim says. "They focused on the positives and made me feel I was up to the challenge. My parents were my heroes."

As Jim grew older, kids got bolder. And meaner. At recess one day, a few boys approached Jim, focused on his arm.

"Did you get bit by a shark?" one kid joked. "You look like Captain Hook!"

Everyone cracked up.

The jokes had become more hurtful, and Jim no longer felt like laughing along.

Sometimes Jim wanted to run away. In second grade, after a recess in which his classmates paid more attention than usual to his prosthetic hand, Jim told his teacher he wasn't feeling well.

"I think I have a fever," the young boy said, pointing to his prosthetic hand.

The teacher wasn't buying it.

"Oh, *really*?"

She didn't let him go anywhere.

Jim decided he'd suffered enough at the expense of his awkward prosthetic limb. Eventually, he convinced his parents to let him ditch the artificial arm and hand. Without the clunky metal prosthesis, Jim found it easier to maneuver through the halls without knocking into things. It also was a relief not to lug the hot metal arm around.

But classmates began focusing on his short right arm, which ended close to where his wrist would have been. Jim wasn't born with a hand or any fingers, but at the end of his right arm was a nubbin, or a tiny mini finger that never fully developed.

Jim's parents and teachers worked with him on a strategy to deal with the questions and confrontations. Soon, Jim was ready with an answer for nosy classmates.

"I was born this way," Jim would respond.

That usually shut most of the kids up. Eventually, the majority of his classmates stopped paying attention to Jim and his difference. They got used to Jim's missing hand, and he got better at ignoring the stares.

The problem was, Mike and Kathy were trying their best to make a living, so they kept moving to nearby cities, seeking better careers and a better life. With each move, Jim was forced to enroll in a new school and meet new kids.

Jim usually buried his right arm deep in his pocket, hoping he'd avoid notice. But when the recess bell rang, there was only so much he could do to avoid the barrage of comments he knew were on the way, some curious, others cruel.

"What happened to you?"

"Can you move it? Does it hurt?"

"Your hand looks like a foot."

"You look like you're giving me the finger!"

Jim just wanted to blend in, to be accepted like everyone else. As he got older, he realized there was just one place he didn't feel like an oddity: the playing field.

From an early age, Jim enjoyed sports. After a long day at school, he would grab a rubber-coated baseball and take aim at a strike zone outlined in chalk on the side of his house. For hours Jim fired away, imagining he was a major-league pitcher.

Along the way, he taught himself to adjust to his physical difference. Before each pitch, Jim would rest his Dusty Baker model glove on the end of his right forearm and throw with his left hand. He'd immediately slip his left hand into the mitt, in time to field the ball. Then Jim would secure the glove between his right arm and his body, take the ball out with his left hand, and fire it, throwing the imaginary runner out.

After a while, switching the glove back and forth became more natural. With help from teachers and others, Jim also figured out how to tie his laces, make a knot, and do other everyday tasks. Without fingers on his right hand, Jim would drop objects and get frustrated sometimes. But he was figuring things out, even how to shake hands by employing a crossover, backhanded grip with his left hand.

Soon, it became obvious Jim wasn't just like his friends—when it came to sports, his abilities were far superior. Jim's left arm was so strong and powerful, and he was such a good athlete that he was chosen as the quarterback or starting pitcher in almost every game.

Jim still dealt with deep insecurities. *How can I have a regular life? Will a girl ever like me?* But on the basketball court, playground, or ball field, the doubts dissipated.

"I could always throw; it was natural for me," Jim says.

Something seemed to push him when he played.

"I thought success would help bring acceptance; that was one of my strongest motivations to play sports," he says. "It gave me self-esteem when I wasn't so sure of myself, and I loved the camaraderie it brought."

Jim began to gain notice for his pitching. When he was twelve, a local newspaper wrote a story about him: "Jimmy Abbott: Special in More Ways Than One." With each victory, he wanted more.

"It was a tad unhealthy," Jim says. "It was too fragile; my self-value depended on success."

But there was something bothering Jim—he didn't want to be known as a good ballplayer, "considering," as Jim puts it, or just for someone who was physically different. He wanted to gain the respect of teammates, coaches, and others simply because he was a talented ballplayer, as good—if not better—than anyone else, regardless of his difference. But he wasn't always sure that's why he was being cheered.

"I didn't want people focusing on my hand; I wanted my play to be first and foremost," Jim says.

Eventually, Jim found himself thinking about his difference less frequently. When he was in school or running around and playing with his friends, he was just like everyone else. His classmates didn't seem to care or even notice.

"As I grew older, I became more comfortable, and it became less of an issue," he says. "I was accepted."

Sports played a huge role in building Jim's confidence.

Even with his newfound attitude, opponents still reminded Jim of his difference. When Jim was twelve, he was pitching during a Little League game one day and heard the opposing coach scream to his batter: "Bunt the ball!" Jim had taught himself to handle ground balls by throwing a baseball against his brick wall and fielding it when it bounced back. But he hadn't yet mastered fielding a slowly bunted ball. Now the coach was taking advantage.

"I wasn't really sure of myself in the field," Jim says.

The first batter bunted the ball, and Jim fumbled it. Safe at first. The coach's plan worked, encouraging him to stick with it.

"Bunt it! Bunt it!" the coach yelled to the next batter.

He ordered the next *seven* batters to bunt on Jim. Each time the batter squared to bunt, Jim was nervous. He knew the coach saw his missing right hand as a weakness. So did everyone in the stands. But now, Jim was getting the hang of it. Each time the ball was bunted, Jim ran to the baseball, scooped it up, and smoothly threw each batter out. Finally, the opposing coach gave up, realizing his plan had backfired.

Over time Jim perfected a strategy to field bunts and ground balls. Sometimes, he pounced on the ball and threw it with his bare left hand so quickly he didn't need to use his glove. On harder-hit balls, Jim would switch his glove to his left hand, field the ball, jam the glove between his chest and armpit, take the ball out with his left hand, and throw the runner out. Opponents challenged Jim so many times that he eventually emerged as the best fielding pitcher in the league.

Early in his life, Jim played sports to fit in. He was the nice kid, laughing along with the jokes, hoping the stares shifted to something or someone else. But as he progressed through high school, Jim played for another reason: to prove he was better than his fellow competitors. On the field, he could turn the tables and show off his mean-spirited side.

"Sports were a way to fight back," he says.

By the time Jim graduated Flint Central High School, he was a standout pitcher who'd finished the year with a super-slim earned run average (ERA) of 0.76. He had a hard fastball, a natural cutter, and developing off-speed pitches. Jim struck out an average of two batters an inning during his senior year and even batted .427

as the team's cleanup hitter. At six foot three, 180 solid pounds, Jim was impressive enough to be drafted in the thirty-sixth round by the Toronto Blue Jays in the 1985 Major League Baseball Draft, but he elected to go to college at the University of Michigan.

Jim's college career began with a couple of rocky starts. A little while later, in a game against rival University of North Carolina, Jim took the mound as a relief pitcher with the game on the line. Tie game, two out, runner on third. Just as the catcher threw the ball back to him, Jim heard the third-base coach for the North Carolina Tar Heels yelling at the top of his lungs.

"Go, go, go!"

The coach was telling the runner to steal home plate on Jim. Once again, an opponent saw Jim's physical difference, assumed he couldn't play at a high level, and decided to try to take advantage. It was a stinging reminder for Jim of how others viewed him.

"I was different, always would be," he says. "With everyone watching in Division I ball, it was unsettling."

Jim was caught by surprise, but his instincts took over. He caught the ball from the catcher, executed his glove switch, and threw home. The runner was out by ten feet. Michigan's bench erupted. Jim won his first college game that day, passing his most important test yet.

In the back of his mind, though, Jim wondered, What did fans and his teammates think? Were they wondering why Michigan had recruited a player with only one hand? If a pitcher with two hands had made the same play would the cheers have been as loud? Even as the awards piled up during his college career, Jim couldn't shake nagging doubts that he was gaining recognition as a curiosity as much as for his pitching.

Jim was chosen by the California Angels with the eighth pick in the 1988 amateur draft, receiving a two-hundred-thousand-dollar signing bonus. Jim's cutter had both serious velocity and enough late movement to make scouts drool. Most people in the baseball world felt he had a bright future in the big leagues.

But Jim noticed some sports analysts and reporters still focused on his physical difference. At his introductory press conference, a reporter asked, "So, Jim, any other handicaps in the family?"

The headline the next day in the *New York Times*: "Angels Get Abbott, One-Hand Pitcher."

Typically, most players spend some time in the minor leagues, trying to hone their game before being sent up to the major-league club. Jim made it to the majors quickly. Probably too quickly. The Angels were a bad team, and when one of their starters got hurt in spring training before the 1989 season, Jim was inserted into the starting rotation. He was still working on his slider and hadn't pitched an inning of minor-league ball, but the Angels needed him. Jim began the 1989 season with two losses.

As the season wore on, he continued to have his share of rough starts. Other times, he seemed to find his stride. All in all, he ended up 12–12 with a respectable 3.92 ERA.

By April 1991, Jim had a 22–30 record in the majors and a lackluster ERA of 4.34. He wasn't fulfilling his promise and felt tension building. He hadn't been given time to mature in the minor leagues and now was wilting under the pressure of the major leagues. Scott Boras, Jim's high-powered agent, encouraged him to see a sports psychologist. Jim resisted the idea at first but finally agreed to go.

They talked about Jim's childhood. They discussed his physical difference and how he used baseball to gain acceptance. If Jim were a star on the field, maybe people wouldn't call him names. Eventually, with the help of his psychologist, Jim began feeling more confident about himself.

"I realized that I didn't have to apologize for the way I was born," Jim says. "I don't need to make others feel good about it. All that matters is I am good with it."

The doctor gave Jim a copy of Cormac McCarthy's classic book *All the Pretty Horses*, in which a character is missing two fingers on a hand due to a shooting accident.

He committed a line in the book to memory:

"Those who have endured some misfortune will always be set apart but that it is just that misfortune which is their gift and which is their strength."

The line spoke to Jim.

"Yes, it's been tough at times," he says, regarding his difference. "But it's such a *gift*."

Jim was maturing as a person and a pitcher. In 1991, Jim won eighteen games with a slim 2.89 ERA, finishing third in the voting for the American League Cy Young Award. The next year, he lowered his ERA to an even stingier 2.77. The best part: Fans, the media, and others viewed him as just another pitcher. Well, not just any old pitcher—a great one. Not a peculiarity. Not someone doing well, considering.

Jim had transformed into a major-league star.

"Let's work outside more and mix in more breaking pitches," New York Yankees pitching coach Tony Cloninger told Jim before a game against the Cleveland Indians on September 4, 1993. There was about a month left before the play-offs were scheduled to begin, and the Yanks were just two games behind the division leading Toronto Blue Jays and needed a win.

The Yankees had traded two promising players to get Jim before the 1993 season. He had mixed success that season, but something about this game seemed different. Early on, Jim threw a curveball to Cleveland Indians slugger Albert Belle that Belle swung at and missed by at least eight inches. It wasn't just Belle who'd been having a hard time dealing with Jim's pitching that day—Jim Thome, who would end his career with 612 home runs, could only manage a lazy fly ball that Bernie Williams easily corralled in center.

Going into the fourth inning, Jim hadn't given up a hit.

In the dugout, he tried to focus on the next batters.

Twenty-seven thousand fans roared. Jim saw his wife, Dana, sitting behind home plate, twenty rows up.

"My battle between innings was to quiet my mind, let go of what already happened and the anxiety of what might happen," he says.

Jim kept on rolling.

Cleveland's speedy center fielder Kenny Lofton fanned on a called strike three in the sixth inning. Designated hitter Manny Ramirez, a future superstar, swung over a changeup for a big strikeout in the seventh.

"The Indians are still hitless," Yankees television broadcaster Tony Kubek told his growing audience.

Usually, when a pitcher is on his way to pitching a no-hitter, his teammates try to avoid calling attention to the fact. But one of Jim's teammates decided to break tradition. As he ran to take his position at first base, Yankees legend Don Mattingly gave Jim a friendly poke in the gut. *He knows,* Jim thought. *They all know.*

Near the end of the game, after Yankees third baseman Wade Boggs lunged to his left and threw Belle out to end another inning without a hit, Jim broke into an exaggerated jog on his way back to the dugout. He was imitating fellow Yankee pitcher Scott Kamieniecki and cracking up his teammates. Jim was having a blast.

Three outs to go. In the dugout, Jim's heart was beating so hard he wondered how he was going to manage to throw a pitch in the ninth. The first batter, Lofton, hit a ball over Jim's head, heading for center field. Just then, Yankees second baseman Mike Gallego swooped in to pick up the ball and threw Lofton out by a half step. The next batter took Jim to the warning track in deep left-center, but Williams, the great Yankees center fielder, tracked the ball down and came up with the catch.

Two outs. The last batter of the game.

Yankee Stadium buzzed with nervous excitement.

Slick-hitting Indians infielder Carlos Baerga was the only thing standing between Jim and a no-hitter. Jim threw Baerga a slider and he pounded it into the ground. Shortstop Randy Velarde was right there, easily throwing Baerga out.

The fans went wild! Jim's teammates raced to the mound to mob him. Jim had pitched a no-hitter, only the sixth ever by a Yankee in their home ballpark.

"Yeah, baby! Yeah, baby!" Jim screamed at the bottom of the pile of exuberant Yankees.

After the game, Mattingly said he'd had goose bumps as he'd pulled for Jim in the ninth alongside fans and teammates.

Jim had risen to the occasion and proven that, despite his physical difference, he was capable of turning in one of the most remarkable performances any pitcher has ever recorded. He showed he was more than a good pitcher, "considering." After all, one-handed guys don't throw no-hitters. Great pitchers do.

Jim had mixed success over the next several years. His fastball went from powerful to pedestrian and he couldn't figure out why. Jim had to rely on his off-speed pitches, still impressing teammates along the way.

"He was a special talent," says Hall of Fame first baseman Frank Thomas, who played with Jim in 1998 on the Chicago White Sox. "He'd hit us with that right hand and it hurt; he was strong. That loosened us up. If he was comfortable with the hand, then we would be, too."

When he was booed and met with failure, Jim realized there was a silver lining.

"It was ironic; my whole life, I wanted to be treated like everyone else," he says. "I found in failure I got that."

The losses hurt Jim's self-confidence. After retiring,

Jim was plagued by questions. With pitching gone, who was he now?

"The foundation I had relied on had crumbled," he says. "It hurt a lot."

Jim was learning a bitter lesson: All kinds of people face crises and self-doubt, not just those with physical differences.

It took a while, but Jim figured out he was more than just a star pitcher. He was a father. He was a husband. And he had a lot to contribute. Jim began giving speeches to young people and adults, sharing lessons learned from the challenges he had overcome.

He told kids not to worry about what others think of their differences.

"You don't have to make anyone feel comfortable," Jim says. "And your success and failure don't change how you should feel about yourself."

One day, Jim came to the classroom of his youngest daughter, Ella, on Career Day to discuss his career and how he had overcome a birth defect to become a star.

After a dozen classmates asked questions, Ella, then five years old, asked one of her own.

"Dad, do you like your little hand?"

The question was so unexpected that Jim didn't

know how to answer. He thought about it for a moment as the class watched. Memories of the shiny, clunky metal hook, the taunts, the ignorance, and the unwanted attention came rushing back. But having a physical difference had spurred Jim to greatness. Being different was special. It made him who he was.

"I do, honey," Jim eventually told his daughter and her classmates. "I haven't always liked it. And it hasn't always been easy. But it has taught me an important lesson: Life isn't easy, and it isn't always fair. But if we can make the most of what we've been given and find our way of doing things, you wouldn't believe what can happen."

ALTHEA GIBSON

Althea Gibson was one of the greatest tennis players who ever lived. She was the first black person to win a Grand Slam Tournament and won both Wimbledon and the US Open in back-to-back years. Althea became a role model for future champions, including Venus and Serena Williams, not only for her athletic excellence, but also for her trailblazing efforts that helped break down long-standing racial barriers.

Before she could set any records or change history, however, Althea had to learn some hard lessons, both in and out of the classroom.

Growing up in the late 1930s in Harlem, Althea attended PS 136 elementary school. Well, she was *supposed* to attend that school in Upper Manhattan. Too often, Althea skipped class in search of adventure.

There were softball games in Central Park, pickup basketball games on local courts, and even boxing matches against older kids. Althea excelled at almost every sport but she paid little attention to her schoolwork.

"I played it all—basketball, shuffleboard, badminton, volleyball," she recalled. "Mama could never get me up from the street. I was down there from morning to night."

In middle school, Althea continued ditching classes. She just didn't see any purpose in showing up.

"My friends and I used to regard school as just a good place to meet and make our plans for what we would do all day," she once said.

Althea wasn't a bad girl. She simply was an independent spirit who craved excitement and became annoyed when teachers or others gave her directions.

"I didn't like people telling me what to do," she said in the book *Born to Win*.

But Althea began getting into more serious trouble. She and her friends skipped school to hop on subways and catch shows at the famed Apollo Theater. They also snuck into movie theaters and stole ice cream and other sweets.

Once, a policeman caught Althea with a stolen sweet

potato. After a lot of pleading and begging, Althea managed to convince the cop to let her go. That wasn't enough to scare her away, though. On a dare from a friend, Althea returned to the store and grabbed another potato, this time without getting caught. She and her friends celebrated the heist by roasting the potato on burning crates in a nearby lot.

When she actually made it back to school, Althea received painful paddlings from teachers and administrators. The punishments had little impact on her attendance, and Althea's father, Daniel, grew furious. Daniel, who was a mechanic, sometimes hit Althea with a strap, a belt, or an ironing cord. He also slapped her with an open hand, as many fathers did at that time. But Althea ignored his building anger. Nothing could get her to focus on her studies.

"I kept running away from home . . . even though I took some terrible whippings for it," Althea later wrote.

One day when she was a teenager, after Althea blew off school several days in a row and swaggered home after hanging out with her friends, her father was about ready to explode. Daniel, a muscular man just shy of two hundred pounds, decided to teach his daughter a hard lesson.

"When I finally showed up," Althea said, "he just walked up to me and punched me right in the face and knocked me sprawling."

He hit Althea so hard that day that the tall, skinny girl went flying down the hall in the family's five-room walk-up. Althea absorbed the blow and picked herself up. She didn't cry or shout. In fact, she didn't utter a single word. Instead, she walked right up to her father and hit him straight in the jaw, as hard as she could.

Althea was clearly a rebellious child, stubborn in her ways. Despite the threats of violence, she wasn't going to change for her father—or for anyone else. "My parents were doing their best work to raise me, but I wouldn't let them," Althea later said. "I just wanted to play, play, play."

Yet Althea cared for her family, despite all the fighting and arguing. As much as she caused them grief, she also looked out for them. One day, she saw the leader of a tough local gang going through the pockets of her uncle Junie, who was slightly drunk and sitting on nearby apartment steps. Althea ran right toward them, trying to stop the theft.

"That's my uncle!" Althea yelled at the gang leader. "Go bother somebody else if you got to steal, but don't bother him!"

Althea helped her uncle to his feet. Upset, the gang leader responded by throwing a sharpened screwdriver straight at Althea. She stuck out her hand, protecting her face, but suffered a serious gash that left a scar on her thumb the rest of her life. After walking her uncle home, Althea fumed. She took off to find the gang leader, fighting him to a draw in a bloody bout that became the talk of the neighborhood.

"He fought me with his fists and his elbows and his knees and even his teeth," Althea said. "He didn't even think of me as a girl, I can assure you. Sometimes, in a rough neighborhood, you've got to let them know you can look out for yourself before they will leave you alone."

As Althea got older, her disobedience grew worse. She continued to cut class and act out like she always had, but her bad behavior escalated. Althea sometimes spent weeks away from school, bored with the courses in her trade school, such as sewing class. For a while, child welfare officials placed Althea in a home for disobedient girls as a ward of the state. She began riding the subways all night, from one end to the other, hiding from truant officers and her own father.

"I was afraid to go home because my father was going to beat me up," she explained.

• • •

Althea was headed down a dangerous path. Luckily for her, the course of her life changed when she met someone who believed in her.

One day, while Althea was playing a version of tennis called paddle tennis on a small neighborhood court, a local musician named Buddy Walker saw her in action, growing more impressed the longer he watched. Buddy became convinced Althea could excel at tennis if given a chance, and that playing the sport could help her grow up and meet "a better class of people," she later recalled. He understood that Althea needed some positive influences around her if she was going to mature and avoid more serious troubles.

Buddy went to a secondhand store and paid five dollars for a used tennis racket and gave it to Althea, encouraging her to hit balls against the wall of a nearby handball court. Later, Buddy took Althea a few blocks away to the Harlem River Tennis Courts so she could play for the first time on an actual tennis court.

From the first stroke, Althea seemed a natural, volleying and serving with ease. Back home, someone strung a net across painted lines of asphalt on the sidewalk of her family's apartment building. Althea and her friends found tennis rackets and began playing— Althea proving to be too much for the others to handle. She trounced all the girls in her neighborhood. Later on, some boys challenged her, boasting that she didn't stand a chance at beating them. Althea overpowered them all; the boys couldn't even return her serves.

Althea began taking lessons from a local tennis pro, thanks to the help of some neighbors, and started playing on courts around the city. But few members of the New York tennis community gave her much respect. Althea was a tall, gangly black kid in a period when African Americans were considered less talented than whites, in sports and in other areas of life. There had never been a black tennis star, let alone a champion. Regulars laughed when they first saw her step on the court.

When Althea began beating almost everyone, the snickering quickly stopped. Before long, she turned cocky, sure she could trounce anyone who dared challenge her. Althea showed little respect for her competitors or for tennis etiquette. Tennis was considered a sport for ladies and gentlemen—a game of culture and politeness.

"I wasn't quite the tennis type," she admitted. "I

kept wanting to fight the other player every time I started to lose."

Althea's confidence masked deep insecurities, friends said. She was skinny and could be awkward away from the court. Althea told one person she was the ugliest in her group of friends. Behind her back, friends made fun of how she played football and baseball with boys, something few girls did at the time.

"It used to hurt me real bad to hear the girls talking about me when they saw me doing that," she later said. "I was the wildest tomboy you ever saw."

After a year of high school, Althea dropped out to live with a family in New York and earn money by working various jobs. School just wasn't for her, she decided, and she wished she had some money in her pockets. Althea continued improving on the court and won her first tournament, the 1942 New York State Open Championship. She figured, *Who needs school when you can beat everyone so easily?*

Success made Althea even brasher and less interested in taking advice from others, including her coaches. She played tournaments around the country and gained supporters in the black community and elsewhere. Althea was convinced she was going to win and often let her opponents know it, too. Once, after whipping rivals in a tournament, Althea didn't bother to shake hands with Nana Davis, the runner-up. Instead, Althea headed straight into the stands to threaten a kid who had been heckling her.

Some opponents started losing patience with Althea. "She had the idea she was better than anybody," Davis said.

As Althea began playing better and older competitors, though, she started losing matches. Even girls with less talent sometimes beat her. They seemed more dedicated to the sport and more determined to improve their game. Althea lacked their discipline and commitment.

Althea didn't rely on strategy and was unprepared for some of her older opponents' clever maneuvers. In the finals of one tournament, a university teacher named Roumania Peters acted exhausted, as if she couldn't even finish the match. Peters dragged herself around the court "as though she was so tired she couldn't stand up," Althea said. "I thought I had it made."

But once she had lulled Althea into complacency, Peters began turning up the heat, beating Althea in three sets and shocking the crowd. Althea was caught unprepared and overconfident. After the match, supporters turned on her, telling Althea she had let them down. They had had enough of her aloof attitude and cocky behavior.

After losing to Peters, Althea sat in the stands, all alone. "It was life's darkest moment," she said.

Althea's talent had taken her a long way, but she wasn't nearly where she wanted to be in her career and life. Two black doctors from the neighborhood remained in Althea's court, though. They offered to help her rebound from the humiliation, but only if she changed her ways. She'd have to move to Wilmington, North Carolina, to live with a new family, they told her. And Althea would have to finish school and improve her behavior.

Althea was scared. She wasn't good at school. And she had heard stories of how blacks were mistreated in the South, sometimes in much worse ways than in the North. Her own family supported her tennis career but was unsure she should move so far away.

Althea asked a famous friend, boxer Sugar Ray Robinson, what she should do. Robinson, who some would later call the best boxer of all time, urged Althea to move south and return to school.

"You'll never amount to anything just banging

around from one job to another like you've been doin'," Ray told Althea. "No matter what you want to do, tennis or music or what, you'll be better at it if you get some education."

Althea was nineteen years old. But she had missed so many classes and had so few credits she was set to be placed in sixth grade at her new school. Attending school as a tall, older girl sitting next to twelve-year-olds promised to be the ultimate humiliation. But Althea's supporters talked the principal into placing her in tenth grade, hoping she could handle the classes and that she'd become more serious about her studies and her life.

Althea immediately faced obstacles in her new and complicated situation. She loved to sing and tried out for the school's choir but gave up when her deep voice made it difficult to blend in. She switched to the boys' section, but everyone laughed at her so she quit.

That was nothing compared to the racism Althea encountered. Back then, discrimination was much more acceptable and commonplace in the United States. Segregation meant blacks had to sit in the back of buses, were forbidden to use the same water fountains as whites, were barred from certain hotels, and suffered through countless acts of oppression. Blacks also didn't receive the same education and employment opportunities.

During her time in the South, Althea confronted such hatred firsthand. While living in North Carolina, she was often forced to change clothes in a car because some country clubs wouldn't let her use their locker rooms. One time, Althea bought a hot dog at a local store but wasn't allowed to sit and eat it at the counter. At the movies, ushers forced her and her black friends to sit in the balcony. When Althea got on a local bus one day and paid her fare, she looked up to see an unsettling sign: *Whites in front, Colored in the rear.* Althea became furious and decided to sit as close to the front of the bus as the rules allowed.

"It disgusted me, and it made me feel ashamed," Althea said.

This time, Althea didn't run away or rebel. She knew she didn't have too many chances left. She was determined to improve her tennis game and try to stay out of trouble.

For Althea, paving a way to a brighter future was a stronger form of rebellion.

Althea forced herself to focus on her studies, and a surprising thing happened—she began to enjoy learning. Her classes were more interesting than she ever expected, and her grades were better than she ever imagined. Althea recognized that it could be fun and even exciting to get the best grades in class, just like it was thrilling to beat opponents on the court. Her change in attitude was likely aided by the fact that she was far from some of her old friends and the distractions of New York.

Althea was named captain of her school's girls' basketball team, played saxophone in the band, and became a model student. She didn't just graduate high school in June 1949—Althea finished *tenth* in her entire class. It was a dramatic change from just a few years earlier, when she couldn't bear to sit in a classroom.

That fall, Althea began college, attending the Florida Agricultural and Mechanical School in Tallahassee, Florida. She joined a sorority and was picked to lead a student disciplinary committee that enforced school rules. She had to laugh; *Althea*, of all people, was the one making sure others obeyed the rules! It was a sign of how far she had come and how much she had changed.

"She was serious, just like she was on the tennis court," said Althea's friend Edwina Martin.

• • •

It wasn't just Althea's academics that were improving— her tennis game was, too. There were still other barriers in Althea's way, though. At the time, there was an unwritten rule that said blacks weren't allowed to compete in tennis's premier events, including the national lawn championship that took place in Forest Hills, New York (now known as the US Open), or other key tournaments sponsored by the United States Lawn Tennis Association (USLTA).

Such discriminatory policies had existed for decades, throughout all major sports. In Althea's day, though, people started to demand change. Jackie Robinson had made his Major League Baseball debut in 1947 with the Brooklyn Dodgers, becoming the first African American professional baseball player. The professional tennis world was a final frontier for African Americans. But the sport wasn't ready to embrace a black player yet, especially a female one.

Earlier in her life, Althea likely would have reacted by lashing out with anger. But she didn't think that approach would spark change. Instead, she decided to prove to the naysayers that she deserved to play on the same court as every other pro. Althea carried herself with a quiet dignity and patiently waited for her chance, hoping it would come.

"I just let all of that roll off my back like water and put my game together as best as I could," Althea said.

Slowly, as she excelled in smaller tournaments, Althea gained backers. Some of the top tennis players thought it was time for a black woman to get a chance to play in the best tournaments. They believed Althea was the perfect candidate to break the color barrier.

Alice Marble, a white four-time national champion, wrote a letter in the July 1950 issue of *American Lawn Tennis* magazine criticizing the United States Lawn Tennis Association's delay in giving Althea permission to play. She wrote that Althea "is not being judged by the yardstick of ability, but by the fact that her pigmentation is somewhat different."

When Althea's application for the US National Tournament was received on August 16, 1950, it received a mention in the *New York Times*, a sign that her efforts were picking up momentum and she was gaining respect. The nation watched and waited to see what the association would do.

The grass court in Forest Hills was fast, an ideal surface for Althea's big serve and quick reflexes. And some pros, like Marble, thought it was time for a black woman to gain an invitation to play in the tournament, especially someone as talented as Althea. But some doubted the tennis establishment was ready for Althea. "No Negro player, man or woman, has ever set foot on one of these courts," journalist Lester Rodney wrote. "In many ways, it is even tougher . . . than was Jackie Robinson's [challenge when he first stepped out of the Brooklyn Dodgers dugout to try to make it in baseball's major leagues]."

Finally, on August 21, less than a week before the tournament was to begin, the USLTA announced that "Miss Gibson was accepted on her ability" as one of fifty-two women selected for the nationals. A new era for tennis and the nation had begun.

Althea took three trains from Manhattan to Queens and walked three blocks to get to the West Side Tennis Club, the site of the famous US Open court. It was Althea's twenty-third birthday, and she was full of jitters. Photographers swarmed, flashbulbs popped in her face, and reporters shouted questions as Althea prepared for her opening-round match against an opponent from England.

Friends detected racism in how the media and crowds treated her.

"Have courage," her friend Alice told her. "Remember, you're just like the rest of us."

Althea tuned out the distractions and focused on her game. In her first match, Althea beat her opponent 6–2, 6–2, leaving the court beaming.

In her next matchup she faced Louise Brough, the reigning Wimbledon Champion and a former US National Winner. As the match began, some in the crowd of two thousand spectators began screaming disgusting racial slurs.

"Beat the nigger!"

"Knock her out of there!"

Althea lost the first set 6–1. But she wasn't going to let some racists get under her skin and disturb her concentration. Althea began ignoring the yelling and focusing on her game. She found her stride and won the second set 6–3, tying the match.

In the final set, Althea fell behind by three games but stormed back to go ahead 7–6. The crowd went wild, sensing a huge upset.

Just then, lightning streaked across the sky, high above the court. A violent thunderstorm erupted, and the match was suspended.

That night, Althea was a nervous wreck. She hardly slept. Could she overcome the odds—and discrimination—to beat the defending champion?

It was not to be. The next day, the game resumed and Brough came back, winning 9–7. Althea had lost the biggest match of her life.

She tried to treat the loss as a positive. "I don't mind getting beat," Althea wrote in a letter to her friend Alice. "The more I am beaten, the more I will learn."

Althea had played well in Forest Hills, lost to a champion, and impressed everyone with her dignity and remarkable composure. In the eyes of many observers, she already was a champ.

"She won something she can cherish throughout her life, which can never be taken from her," the *New York Herald Tribune* wrote, "the respect and admiration of all who saw her play. . . . She is not only a credit to the Negro race but to all good sportsmen and women who play and love the game of tennis."

She was determined to persevere. In 1951, Althea headed to Wimbledon and became the first black woman to participate in the world's oldest and most prestigious tennis tournament. She arrived in England prepared to deal with twenty thousand potentially hostile fans.

"I made a vow to myself," she recalled. "'Althea, you're not going to look around. You're not going to listen to any calls or remarks. All you're going to do is watch the tennis ball.'"

Just like she had at the US National Tournament, Althea won her first match at Wimbledon but lost in the second round. Despite the loss, she left England with her head held high.

She returned home to resume her studies. She knew school would help her mature and grow as a person and a player. Committed to her education, Althea graduated from college in 1953.

Three years later, Althea made history, winning the French Open, becoming the first African American to win a Grand Slam Tournament. She and her partner also were doubles champs that same year.

Althea was just getting started. After winning the French Open, her focus turned to Wimbledon. Althea entered the tournament in 1957 and resolved to improve on her previous appearance. Some in the crowd cheered her on. Others jeered, unwilling to root for a black champion.

"I'll mess them up on the court, and then the joke will be on them," she said.

England was experiencing an unusually hot summer that year. Over a thousand people had fainted watching tennis over the course of the two-week tournament. Althea persevered, cruising through the opening rounds without losing a single set. The temperature was a sweltering one hundred degrees on the day of the finals. Althea didn't mind the heat. She told herself the heat on the court's surface would help her round strokes, which she relied on to fluster Darlene Hard, a Californian. In only fifty minutes, Althea topped Hard 6–3, 6–2.

"At last! At last!" she cried as the match ended.

Althea Gibson was Wimbledon's Champion, the first black victor in the tournament's eighty-year history. She fought back tears as Queen Elizabeth presented her with a gold trophy.

"Shaking hands with the queen of England was a long way from being forced to sit in the colored section of the bus," she remarked later on in life. It was a sign of how far she had come, as a player and a person.

Back in Harlem, friends, family, and fans hailed her big victory. Althea became the second black athlete, after sprinter Jesse Owens, to be honored with a ticker-tape parade up New York's Canyon of Heroes, in front of a crowd of a hundred thousand people.

Althea would win the US National Championship

that year and repeat as Wimbledon Champion the next year, becoming the first African American to be ranked number one in the world. In all, Althea won fifty-six national and international singles and doubles titles, including eleven Grand Slam Championships, cementing her position as one of the nation's greatest sports legends.

"She had the resilience to be a champion under such challenging circumstances," says tennis superstar Venus Williams. "There wasn't much money in tennis at the time, and she persevered for the love of the game—and the pursuit of social fairness."

After retiring, Althea became a leading advocate for education as well as a university teacher, a final irony for a woman who fled from school and hid from teachers in her youth. Just as important, Althea was a role model for others facing their own challenges, in sports and in life. When Venus Williams and her sister Serena were battling their way to the top of the women's game, they looked to Althea and her story for guidance and inspiration.

"Althea Gibson was a tremendous trailblazer," Venus

says. "I'm very aware that she endured so many hardships to create opportunities for others to play professional tennis."

Venus says she tried to ignore the skeptics, just like Althea.

"Do not let outsiders bring negativity into your mind or your life. . . . I call those people 'dream stealers'—they will try to take your dreams because they are not thinking the same way that you are and they do not have the same confidence that you do. Listen to those who think proactively and focus on improvement."

Venus says she learned other important lessons from Althea, which helped Venus win a remarkable seven Grand Slam Singles Championships, including five Wimbledon titles.

"Identify your strengths and focus on them," Venus says. "Find confidence in what you can do and pour your heart into maximizing those skills."

Venus and Serena both say Althea influenced more than just the world of tennis. "Her greatest accomplishment, in my opinion, is that she affected cultural behavior, political norms, and ultimately legislation throughout the world," Venus says. "Tennis created a platform for her to become a champion in sport and the human rights struggle. There is much more work left to be done, and Serena and I are proud to do our part in keeping Althea Gibson's legacy alive."

Althea made huge strides to help African Americans progress on the road to racial equality. Her dignity and accomplishments—on the court, in the classroom, and elsewhere—sent a message to the rest of the world. She emerged as a force of athletic achievement and shined as a beacon for racial equality. Across the globe, fans and critics alike couldn't help but appreciate the greatness of Althea Gibson.

LEBRON JAMES

In December 1984, Gloria James brought her baby from the hospital to her mother's home, a large and magnificent Victorian on a tree-lined boulevard in South Akron, Ohio. The house had a sizable front porch, a foyer, and a grand living room. A television room and a pantry were on the first floor, and four large bedrooms upstairs. The impressive home, which had been in Gloria's family for generations, once had a blueberry bush and pear trees on its grounds, along with horses and even a goat.

But early on Christmas morning in 1987, LeBron's grandmother died of a massive heart attack. She was forty-two years old. Gloria, who was just nineteen at the time, didn't want to ruin the holiday for her three-year-old son, so she held off on telling LeBron the sad news until he had finished opening his presents, which included a plastic mini basketball hoop that quickly became his favorite toy.

LeBron's grandmother had helped Gloria pay her bills. Without that help, it became much harder for Gloria to meet the family's monthly expenses. Strapped for cash, she took any kind of job she could find, but it was never enough. Their house was majestic, but it also was quite old; the plumbing and electricity were failing, and other costly repairs were desperately needed.

Before long, the city served Gloria with a series of eviction notices demanding that she and LeBron vacate the deteriorating home. Eventually, it was condemned and bulldozed, forcing Gloria and LeBron to search for somewhere to live.

Gloria found a new apartment, but soon they had to leave once again. It became a pattern. Gloria would find a new apartment or house, but a complication would arise or a bill would be ignored and they'd have to pack up. Gloria tried her best. But it usually was only a month or two before she and LeBron were looking for a new home. Between the ages of five and eight, LeBron and his mother moved twelve times.

"We moved from apartment to apartment, sometimes living with friends," LeBron told *ESPN The*

Magazine. "My mom would always say, 'Don't get comfortable, because we may not be here long.'"

When they did find somewhere to live, it usually was in a gritty part of town. LeBron learned to deal with the crime and gangs around him. But it never was easy. While living in a two-story apartment building in the city's Elizabeth Park projects, for example, where dozens of buildings had been condemned or boarded up, sirens and gunfire sometimes kept LeBron up at night, leaving the boy scared, lonely, and worried.

"You lie in bed and you just know something bad is happening, something heavy," LeBron wrote in his book, *Shooting Stars*, "and you just thank the Lord that it isn't you out there."

LeBron was able to endure the difficult times, because he had his mother to love and comfort him. LeBron never knew his father, Anthony, an ex-convict who had checked out when he heard Gloria James had become pregnant with LeBron. But his mother doted on her son, making him feel he had everything he needed.

LeBron rarely grumbled or whined about his unsettled life. At an early age, he learned that complaining only placed more pressure on his mother; he knew she had enough on her shoulders and that she already felt guilty she couldn't keep the family in a home. So

LeBron accepted the circumstances of his life and the need to constantly move around. He began keeping a backpack full of everything he cherished near his bed each night. That way he could just grab the bag and go when his mother said it was time to find a new home. Instead of getting frustrated, LeBron chose to find positive aspects in the difficult situation; being prepared to leave at a moment's notice gave him a feeling of freedom, he decided.

LeBron searched for the positives in other parts of his life, too. He was an only child and at times was lonely. He also felt the need to mature faster than other kids to better deal with his family's challenges. But LeBron grew proud that he was more independent than his friends and could take care of himself.

He discovered a similar feeling of confidence on the basketball court. LeBron started playing basketball around the age of nine, though football was his first love. LeBron played tailback and wore number twenty-one, in tribute to Cleveland Browns speedy running back Eric Metcalf. Playing peewee football, LeBron took his first handoff eighty yards for a touchdown, winning instant popularity with his teammates. LeBron became the star of the team, scoring nineteen touchdowns in six games as a speedy receiver.

Gloria couldn't afford the participation fee, so she volunteered to be the team mother to pay for LeBron's spot, coming to practice, taking attendance, and filling water bottles. As LeBron raced toward a touchdown, his mother often ran down the sideline, stride for stride with her son, rooting him on.

It didn't take long for LeBron to begin enjoying basketball as well. LeBron loved sprinting up and down the court, gambling for steals on defense and converting on breakaway layups. In class, he sketched hundreds of logos of the Dallas Cowboys and Los Angeles Lakers into his school notebook, reflecting his twin loves.

LeBron James's basketball coach, Frank Walker Sr., saw great potential in him, but Coach Walker felt that LeBron was in desperate need of schooling. Coach Walker wasn't content to watch nine-year-old LeBron race up and down the court with little purpose, relying on his right hand for every shot. Coach Walker decided to begin LeBron's education by teaching him how to make a layup with his left hand.

It was a huge challenge. LeBron was a righty, so relying on his left hand to hit a layup seemed just too difficult. He didn't understand why he had to use both hands when his right-handed layup was working so well, and he quickly became discouraged.

"I can't do it," LeBron told his coach one day, saying he wanted to give up.

"He used to cry about it," Coach Walker recalls.

Walker wouldn't let up, though. LeBron and his teammates practiced lefty layups every single day.

When LeBron got frustrated, Coach Walker would say, "You'll be a much better player if you learn how to make shots with both hands."

"You're going to need a left-handed layup one of these days," Walker sometimes added.

He gave LeBron and his teammates a series of challenging drills. Sometimes, they had to put their right hands in their pockets or behind their backs as they quickly dribbled down the court. Other times, Coach Walker had a defender chase LeBron and his teammates downcourt as they went in for left-handed layups. Over time, LeBron learned to ignore aggressive defenders and convert layups with either hand, a unique skill for a boy so young.

Walker told LeBron, who at that point was nearly five foot five inches tall, that he could have a future in basketball if he kept improving and didn't give up so easily. All LeBron needed to do was to stay focused and determined.

Moving from apartment to apartment began to impact both his training and his life, though.

"That kind of life builds up a lack of trust, a feeling that what you care about and the friends you have made will disappear," LeBron says. "You just know that you're going to be on the move, getting that little backpack ready because it's time to roll again."

Constantly changing schools was especially difficult for LeBron, who had trouble making new friends. Parents and coaches noticed he rarely smiled or exhibited joy like others his age.

"The hardest thing for me was going to new schools and meeting new friends and finally getting comfortable with them and then having to leave and go to another school and getting comfortable again and the leaving again," LeBron says. "Over and over, the cycle repeated itself."

One thing LeBron could count on was his mother's emotional support. Her love was a security blanket that comforted LeBron, giving him hope and confidence. But Gloria was a young woman with enormous challenges of her own. As she tried to get her life together and find steady work, she wasn't always around, upsetting her son, whom she called Bron Bron.

"Sometimes I went to bed not knowing if I was going to see her the next morning," LeBron wrote. "I would sometimes go a few nights without seeing her at all. I became afraid that one day I would wake up and she would be gone forever."

LeBron began having real difficulties in school in 1993, when he was in fourth grade. That year, he missed over eighty days of school—half the school year—because he lived too far away and didn't have a reliable way to get to class or anyone pushing him to get to class. LeBron was sleeping on a couch in the one-bedroom apartment of one of his mother's friends. The women liked to host parties that could last late into the night. Sometimes it got so noisy that the police were called to investigate. His mother was on welfare, and there were times LeBron was left to fend for himself. Instead of going to school, he sometimes played video games and headed to the corner store to buy snacks with his mother's food stamps.

LeBron's grades began to suffer. Sports still came easily to him, but even on the football field or basketball court, LeBron didn't laugh very much or seem very happy. He seemed to have too much on his mind, adults said.

"I was on the edge of falling into an abyss from which I could never escape," LeBron says.

One day, LeBron's mother sat him down to share some shocking news: She was sending him to live with Coach Walker and his family. It would just be until his mother was in a financial situation where she could better take care of them, she insisted. LeBron's mother said she hated that he'd be moving away from her but that the decision was for the best.

LeBron knew his mother was making a difficult decision and that she was trying to help him avoid deeper troubles and make something of his life. Still, the nine-year-old was shaken. He worried that it would be hard to adjust to his new family and wondered when he'd see his mother again.

"It was unimaginable," LeBron says. "I had never met my father, and the idea of losing my mother, even if it was temporary, frightened me."

LeBron and his mother hardly knew his new family, adding to his anxiety. Frank and Pam Walker had first met LeBron when he played on a peewee football team called the East Dragons with their son, Frankie Jr. At the time, Frank noticed that LeBron was more serious and shy than the other kids, despite his dominance on the field. All the moving had forced LeBron to mature quickly and assume more responsibility than others his age, it seemed.

When LeBron hadn't returned to school after Christmas break during fourth grade and other parents mentioned that Gloria was looking for a more stable home for her son, the Walkers decided to help, offering to take LeBron into their home to live with them and their three kids.

Others involved in the football team or school had made similar proposals in the past after noting how often LeBron was absent from school. But those offers usually came from single men trying to get their own acts together. The Walkers were a real family, something LeBron never had experienced. His mother sensed that living with Frank and Pam Walker was an opportunity she and her son couldn't pass up.

She hashed out a plan for LeBron to stay with the Walkers during the week and return to her apartment each weekend.

"I don't want to give the impression that Glo just dropped LeBron off on our doorstep," Pam Walker later told *ESPN The Magazine*. "It was important to him and to her that they maintain their relationship. So, wherever she was staying, he went with her on the weekend."

LeBron left to live with the Walkers, worried about how he would fit in. Would the three children want another kid in the house? Early on, Chanelle, the oldest in the family, made it clear she didn't want anything to do with him, adding to his nervousness. But LeBron got along well with her younger sister, Tanesha. And he quickly became close friends with Frankie Jr., sharing a room in the three-bedroom home.

Living with his mother, LeBron often went to sleep around midnight, even on school nights, and had few responsibilities. The Walkers demanded much more of him. Each evening, LeBron was expected to take a shower or bath. Every morning, the Walkers woke the kids up at 6:45 a.m. sharp. LeBron shared a series of chores with the Walker kids; they cleaned the bathrooms and countertops, washed the dishes, swept the floors, and took out the trash. The children kept their rooms neat and made their beds each day. They spoke politely and weren't permitted to talk back. The chores and rules were aimed at teaching the kids to behave respectfully.

LeBron also learned the value of hard work from Frank, who had a job at the Akron Metropolitan Housing Authority, and Pam, who was employed in the office of a local congressman. Pam Walker reminded LeBron that he'd have his pick of scholarships from colleges around the nation if he focused on his schoolwork along with basketball.

Meanwhile, Frank Walker kept working with LeBron, and with his own son, to help them improve their games. To expand LeBron's basketball IQ, Frank enlisted him to work as an assistant when he coached a team of eight-year-olds.

"You could see his skills getting better at Frank's house literally every day," says Bruce Kelker, who once coached LeBron as a boy.

The discipline, high expectations, and stable family life were exactly what LeBron needed. Soon, he began to thrive in the classroom. LeBron realized that he actually enjoyed school when he applied himself. Living with the Walkers during fifth grade, LeBron didn't miss a single day of class, taking particular pleasure in art, music, and gym classes. At the end of that year, LeBron was given the school's attendance award.

"Best award ever," he later told ESPN.

Once, LeBron had been a boy on the edge. His life

had been full of tumult and sadness. But his fifth-grade teacher, Karen Grindall, described him very differently:

"So steady," he recalled in an interview years later. "So happy."

Eventually, Pam Walker helped Gloria find an apartment she could afford in Akron's Springhill apartment complex. Most considered the area ugly and run-down, but it was heaven to LeBron. He had his mother back and even his own room. But the lessons provided by the Walkers would pay dividends for years to come.

Soon, LeBron started attracting attention in Akron, elsewhere in the state, and around the country for his remarkable basketball prowess. Playing on a local AAU team called the Shooting Stars with three close friends from Akron, LeBron led his team to local and national success. LeBron was six feet tall in eighth grade and he could jump higher and shoot with more accuracy than anyone he faced. Few could dribble like he could. Those skills also weren't the biggest reasons LeBron earned national acclaim, however.

Instead, coaches, reporters, and scouts pointed to

LeBron's remarkable maturity and court savvy. It was the kind of poise they usually only saw in players much older and with far more experience than LeBron. Perhaps it was because he had been forced to grow up more quickly than other kids his age. Maybe it was the accountability and responsibility the Walkers instilled in him. Either way, LeBron was calm under pressure and had unmatched court vision. He instantly found open teammates and eagerly shared the ball, a rare trait for a player who also could score at will. Some said he even reminded them of Magic Johnson, the legendary Los Angeles Lakers point guard.

After LeBron and his four friends, nicknamed the "Fab Four," enrolled in a local high school, St. Vincent–St. Mary High School, something remarkable happened that helped LeBron gain even more attention: He kept growing.

"I remember sleeping over at his place [during the summer before tenth grade]," says his friend and high school teammate Sian Cotton. "I swear, he grew two inches overnight!"

By the end of that summer, LeBron was nearly six foot seven inches. A year later, LeBron was invited by Michael Jordan to a private scrimmage in Chicago. Yes, *the* Michael Jordan, the Chicago Bulls legend. Jordan matched LeBron up against NBA pros Jerry Stackhouse and Corey Maggette, competition that likely would have intimidated most high schoolers.

But not LeBron. He held his own against Jordan and the other NBA players.

Later, Jordan told reporters what impressed him the most: LeBron's ambidexterity. He was nearly as good with his left hand as he was with his right. All those grueling drills developed by Frank Walker had paid off.

After the scrimmage, Jordan gave LeBron his cell phone number, a sign of the respect he held for the young man. When he got back home and Frank Jr. heard he had Jordan's number, Frank Jr. grabbed LeBron's phone. Frank and his friends then called the number, according to *ESPN The Magazine*. Jordan picked up, but the boys were too nervous to say anything, so they hung up. It didn't take long for Jordan to change his number.

After his impressive performance against Jordan and the other pros, LeBron's legend began to spread. During his junior year of high school, he averaged nearly thirty points a game and was featured on the cover of *Sports Illustrated* magazine. Some of his games were even broadcast on ESPN, more evidence his star was on the rise.

After graduating high school, LeBron had a tough choice to make—turn pro or go to college? Though players can no longer go directly to the NBA after finishing high school, that rule didn't come into effect until after LeBron faced the decision. At the time, reporters wanted to know if LeBron was having a difficult time making up his mind.

"People ask me if it's a hard decision going to the NBA, but I've made harder decisions," he told a reporter. "Decisions about smoking or going to school, stealing from a store or not stealing. Those are harder decisions."

LeBron was chosen with the first pick in the 2003 NBA Draft by the Cleveland Cavaliers, a team that played just forty miles from his hometown of Akron. It didn't take long for LeBron to show skeptics all the excitement about him was warranted, despite his lack of playing experience at the collegiate level. In his first NBA game, LeBron scored 25 points and had 9 assists and 4 steals.

The Cavaliers lost the game to the Sacramento Kings, but LeBron had given the Cleveland fans something to be excited about. Later that season, he racked up forty-one points in a game. That year, LeBron averaged nearly 21 points, 5.5 rebounds, and almost 6 assists per game on his way to becoming the NBA's Rookie of the Year.

A year later, during the 2004–05 season, LeBron earned his first All-Star selection, the first of eleven straight appearances so far. That year, he also became the youngest player in NBA history to be named to an All-NBA Team, guiding the Cavaliers to their first play-off appearance in almost a decade.

Off the court, LeBron showed signs of maturing into a public leader and personality. He appeared in movies, hosted *Saturday Night Live*, and became a vice president of the National Basketball Players Association.

LeBron left Cleveland for Miami in 2010 in a high-profile signing announced on television with so much hoopla that many thought it was in bad taste, partly because his departure was a crushing blow to fans in his home state. Later, LeBron took responsibility for the mistake.

"I apologize for the way it happened," LeBron said, owning up to his error, another example of the sense of responsibility he had learned early in life.

LeBron continued to dominate the league in subsequent years, becoming one of only five players to win at least four Most Valuable Player Awards (as of 2015). He became a true basketball legend, on par with his own heroes, Michael Jordan and Magic Johnson, winning two NBA Championships with the Miami Heat and earning two finals MVP Awards in those years.

In 2014, LeBron returned home, re-signing with the Cleveland Cavaliers. He was the pride of Akron once again, for both his play and his personality.

Today, when LeBron speaks to students about the year that changed his life, he doesn't point to 2007, the season he led the Cavs to the team's first NBA Championship appearance. He also doesn't mention the four straight years he and the Miami Heat reached the NBA Finals after joining the team in 2010, including the two years he won back-to-back championships in 2012 and 2013. He doesn't discuss the play-off run in 2015, when he led the Cavs to another championships appearance in his first season back on the team.

Instead, LeBron speaks about fourth grade, the year the Walkers changed his life. LeBron has acknowledged many times that the lessons he learned from Frank and Pam Walker provided the foundation for all his remarkable success.

In the spring of 2013, for example, LeBron and the Miami Heat were desperate to win the first game of the Eastern Conference Finals against the Indiana Pacers. As overtime winded down, LeBron drove hard to the basket, winning the game with a difficult, left-handed layup just before the buzzer sounded. It was the second time that season LeBron had won a game with a last-second lefty layup.

After the game, LeBron thanked the man who taught him so many lessons, both on and off the court.

"Frank Walker, my first basketball coach, taught me how to make a left-handed layup," LeBron told reporters. "He wouldn't let me dribble until I got the right steps down and the right [form] to make a left-handed layup consistently."

When asked about LeBron's words of appreciation, Frank Walker gave a simple response: "I'm very proud of what he's done."

The lessons Frank and Pam Walker had imparted were two decades old, but they were still relevant. For LeBron and his many fans throughout the world, it's proof that challenging experiences in youth sometimes result in benefits that last a lifetime.

SHANE BATTIER

Shane Battier seems like a guy who had it made from the day he was born.

Shane grew up in a comfortable, middle-class neighborhood in Birmingham, Michigan, about ten miles from Detroit. His dad ran a successful trucking company, hauling and warehousing steel for the auto industry. For much of Shane's childhood his mom was a stay-at-home parent, helping to raise Shane and his siblings.

From an early age, Shane was taller than all his classmates—and a much better athlete, both bigger and stronger than competitors. As he got older, Shane continued to excel in sports and found a second home on the basketball court.

In college, Shane emerged as a star small forward at Duke University and helped lead his team to victory in the 2001 NCAA Championship. Later that year, the Memphis Grizzlies selected Shane sixth overall in the NBA Draft. He went on to become a solid pro, winning back-to-back NBA Championships with the Miami Heat in 2012 and 2013. After losing in his third straight NBA finals appearance with the Heat the following season, Shane officially retired from the NBA. As soon as his thirteen-year playing career ended, Shane had job offers waiting for him; he slid right into the television booth as an NBA analyst on ESPN.

A life of few challenges and plenty of good fortune, right?

Hardly.

Throughout his childhood, Shane often was socially awkward and anxious. He couldn't find a way to fit in with classmates and became withdrawn and shy.

Then one day Shane had enough of feeling insecure. He made a difficult decision that would change his life.

At a very young age, Shane realized he was very different from those around him. Shane's father was black, and his mother was white. Back in the 1970s and '80s, biracial families weren't nearly as common as they are today. Growing up in a largely white neighborhood,

Shane often noticed his classmates staring at him, focusing on how different his skin color was from theirs. Feeling like an outsider, Shane struggled to fit in.

"I didn't know any kids with parents of different races. I was the only biracial kid," he recalls. "It was my most defining attribute."

Teachers and others often cast an unwanted spotlight on young Shane. One morning in first grade, Shane's teacher announced it was picture day. As the students lined up to have their photos taken, teachers handed out combs so the kids could straighten their hair and look their best. But, like many African Americans, Shane's hair was naturally curly. So when his turn came, he was given a hair pick rather than a comb. When his classmates saw the hair pick, they dissolved into giggles. The embarrassing episode had a lasting impression on Shane—it was a painful moment he would remember for the rest of his life.

A few years later, a teacher stood in front of Shane's class to explain why the school was celebrating Martin Luther King Day. Suddenly, one of Shane's classmates turned to him, screaming out to the entire class.

"You should know everything about MLK, Shane," the classmate said, "because you're black!"

Shane's classmates turned to face him. As they

gawked, Shane struggled to find something to say. The classmate who'd spoken up had made a narrow-minded assumption; just because he had African American roots didn't mean Shane knew everything there was to know about Martin Luther King. And the last thing he wanted was his friends focusing on him, once again, just because of his skin color.

"I'll never forget that," Shane says. "It was a white-bread, upper-middle-class area, there were no other minorities, so it was difficult."

Throughout elementary school, these uncomfortable moments made Shane wish he could simply look like everyone else. As he grew older, Shane's struggles persisted and he found it even harder to blend in. By fourth grade, he'd grown so much that he towered over his classmates. Others might have enjoyed the height advantage, but Shane viewed it as one more way he stood out when he just wanted to fit in.

"I was always different, and I always stuck out," he says.

Shane began to take sports seriously around the age of ten, practicing for hours on the basket in his driveway. In the winter, Shane would wake up early to shovel the driveway and put up some shots. He developed a daily workout routine, which included ball handling, shooting, and other drills, often working with a friend who later became a Navy Seal.

"Every day I would hop on my ten-speed bike and look for a gym or park to get my workouts in," he says.

It quickly became apparent that Shane had special talent. He wasn't just bigger and stronger than his classmates; he was much, much better. When he played basketball, Shane outscored and outrebounded everyone else on the court. He was nearly impossible to guard. Defenders had no chance against him.

"I was a head taller than everyone and very co-ordinated. That led me to become the Dikembe Mutombo of the YMCA league," Shane says, referring to the shot-blocking former NBA legend.

By fifth grade, Shane already was five foot eight and looked much older than his classmates. Even when he played against older kids he didn't face much competition. When he faced kids his own age, it was even less of a challenge.

"It got to the point where even my close friends didn't want to play with me," he says.

Shane sometimes felt his athletic prowess was a hindrance, rather than a help. Being better than everyone else was less fun than anyone could have imagined.

"It was unfair. I felt ostracized," he says.

One day, Shane's coach shared an idea: Why not join the Detroit Police Athletic League downtown to compete against the best kids in the region, including black kids from Detroit's inner city?

Shane was apprehensive. He didn't know anyone in the league and was nervous about meeting new kids. He hadn't spent much time in Detroit. But Shane was developing a true love of basketball and agreed to give it a try, hoping he might finally find a place where he could fit in.

Shane was anxious to see how he would be treated. As he shot around with some kids on one of the first days of practice, a teammate turned to him with a huge grin, as if he was a tourist spotting an unusual sight.

"Hey!" he yelled to all the other kids. "It's a white kid from the suburbs!"

Shane flushed with embarrassment as players howled with laughter. They acted like it was the biggest joke of the year. Even in Detroit, Shane couldn't help standing out. This time he was being targeted because his skin wasn't dark enough for those around him.

Once the season started, Shane showed off his skills

to the rest of the league, scoring and rebounding as well as almost anyone else. The Detroit kids never let him forget where he came from or how different he looked, however. Opponents chirped at Shane as he dribbled or shot, making fun of how much lighter his skin was, trying to throw his game off.

"It was a tough league," he recalls. "They would look at me and talk trash."

Despite the name-calling, Shane kept working on his game, and improving. Shane learned to ignore the insults. He was thrilled when he was selected to play at a prestigious basketball camp in Detroit run by Isiah Thomas, the legendary Detroit Pistons point guard who later would be inducted into the Hall of Fame. It was the kind of camp where future stars sometimes gained notice from scouts, reporters, and others.

On the first day, before camp officially began, Shane was shooting around by himself, minding his own business, when he saw a few kids approaching from the other side of the gym. They were sizing him up. Shane tried to act nonchalant and kept on shooting, waiting for the leader of the group to render a verdict on the newcomer.

It didn't take him long.

"Look at the pretty boy over there with the clean sneakers and cute dimples," he said to his friends, cracking them up.

Shane wasn't sure how to respond. Sure, his parents got him clean basketball gear and a new pair of basketball sneakers each year, partly because he grew so fast he couldn't wear the old ones. He was a typical middle-class kid. Should he feel bad about that? Should he have to defend himself?

"I was used to that stuff, but I didn't know how to react," he says.

In the end, he grabbed his basketball, turned away from the boys, and went back to shooting all by himself. For weeks Shane's basketball outfit would be a source of humor. The Detroit kids saw him as a rich white kid from the suburbs and resented the privileged life they assumed he enjoyed, so they mocked him. Few could have suspected the stress Shane was dealing with.

"I lived in Birmingham; no one could relate to me," Shane says.

Back at school, classmates never poked fun at Shane for his skin color, but he still felt they treated him differently. In sixth grade, for example, Shane asked a girl to go out with him but got rejected. He couldn't tell for sure, but he suspected she turned him down because of the color of his skin.

I'm never going to fit in, he thought.

Shane was uneasy around others and became a loner. He had friends but tended to be withdrawn, worried that classmates were judging him, just like the Detroit kids. Was he acting too white? Too black? He began doubting himself. To Shane, it felt as though neither the white community nor the African American community would fully accept him. He took it hard.

"As a kid, you want to be liked and loved and fit in," Shane says. "But there was no one like me. I didn't feel I fit in. I struggled with my confidence."

His parents tried to be supportive, saying all the right things.

"You're a great person," his mother often said. "That's all that matters."

"It doesn't matter what people say about you," his father would add.

But even though they were on his side, Shane didn't feel comfortable sharing the upsetting details of his troubles with his parents.

"I never talked about my struggles with anyone [and] my parents didn't know the extent of my issues,"

Shane says. "They were going through their own issues as an interracial couple in the 1980s. Most people couldn't relate to what I was going through and I
didn't know anyone [dealing with similar issues]."

Shane felt just as awkward about the idea of approaching others with his problem. He didn't have
much of a relationship with his mother's family, many
of whom weren't pleased she had married an African
American man. He wasn't close with his father's family, either. With no one to turn to, Shane kept his frus-
trations and insecurities bottled up.

"I kept it all inside; I've always been extremely independent," he says. "I knew my parents loved me,
and they reiterated that I was a good person. But there
was nothing they could do to help me."

Shane was determined to find his own way in life.

There was one place where Shane always felt comfort: the basketball court. Whenever he felt down
or alone, he picked up a ball, grabbed his basketball
sneakers, and headed to the nearest court. He often
played by himself, using the time to improve his skills,
working on his shot, his moves, and his overall game.

Shane poured his emotions and feelings into his
play and found relief, shot after shot, swish after
swish, feeling more confident with each bucket. A

smile would form on his face, and he kept coming back for more.

"Basketball didn't care what my race was or where I lived or how I talked or acted," he says. "I was always super motivated to work on my game. I lost myself in the game and developed a passion and love for it."

Shane continued to play ball in Detroit leagues, doing his best to block out the teasing. He had good grades, and his coaches and teachers said he had a shot at playing basketball at a top university. A basketball magazine even named him the fourth-best seventh grader in the country.

Shane kept returning to the basketball court, turning his shyness and emotional upheaval into an advantage. The more solo practice sessions he had, the more his game improved. He found solace in a place he felt he truly belonged.

Eventually, Shane saw that being alone on the court wasn't such a bad thing.

"I knew I was lucky I had basketball; that was my outlet," he says. "I realized I didn't need anything else."

One day, as an upperclassman in high school, Shane decided he'd had enough of worrying about how others viewed him. It was no fun being embarrassed all the time. If neither the white community nor the African American community would fully embrace him, that was fine. He'd carve out his own place in the world. There was no eureka moment or experience that changed it all for Shane. It wasn't something anyone said to him. He just stopped caring about what other people thought of him.

Apologetic and nervous is no way to go through life, he concluded.

"It was just me," he says. "I finally said, 'You know what, I'm a good person who tries to treat people the right way. If people don't like me because of how I live or how I look, that's their loss.'"

Almost immediately, it was like a heavy weight had lifted off Shane's shoulders. He finally felt good about himself. Instead of being ashamed he wasn't completely white or black, Shane decided that being of mixed race gave him all kinds of advantages others didn't have.

"I can fit in everywhere," he says. "I am the all-American mutt, and I'm proud of it."

All the hard work on the court began to pay off, as did Shane's newfound perspective on life. Shane graduated from Detroit Country Day School in 1997, receiving the Naismith Award as the best high-school basketball player in the entire nation. To cap it all off,

Shane was recruited by Duke University, one of the most distinguished universities in the country, known for its excellent academics and elite basketball program.

At Duke, playing for legendary Coach Mike Krzyzewski, better known as Coach K, Shane met kids with similar experiences. "I [finally] met [other] biracial kids who were comfortable [with] who they were," he says. "I became really confident and proud of my background."

Now that Shane didn't care what others thought about him, he realized the same was true with respect to his play on the court. Just as he finally was unapologetic about who he was as a person and didn't care that he didn't look like others, Shane also stopped caring about how he looked on the basketball court. He became willing to do the dirty work in games—the types of things others players weren't eager to do—partly because they feared they wouldn't look cool.

When an opponent barreled into the lane, for example, Shane held his ground, taking painful, ugly charges. He worked on his defense, rather than highlight-reel dunks, becoming one of the top defensive players in the NCAA Division I Men's Basketball League.

Once, Shane had been a shy, nervous boy who preferred to play basketball alone. Now he was a young man who excelled in the college game and emerged as a leader. He no longer was the quiet guy on the court; instead he helped to call out defensive instructions to teammates, handing out pointers and gaining their respect. During his time at Duke, Shane won a record-tying 131 college-basketball games, including the 2001 NCAA Men's Basketball Championship. That same year, he was named the best college basketball player in the country, winning the AP College Player of the Year Award, the Naismith College Player of the Year Award, and the John R. Wooden Award.

In 2001, Shane was selected by the Memphis Grizzlies with the sixth pick in the first round of the NBA Draft and began his pro career as a six-foot-eight forward.

Shane quickly saw he had a serious problem, however. He realized that most players in the league were even better athletes than he was, making it difficult for Shane to become a star. In the NBA, almost everyone can hit an open jump shot or dunk on a smaller defender— those feats might've been more remarkable in the college game where Shane had excelled, but this was a whole new class of talent. He couldn't dribble as well as most guards and forwards, often had his shot blocked, and seemed a step slower than most opponents. Clearly Shane was at a big disadvantage. A lot was expected of him as a first-round pick from a prestigious college program, and he wasn't sure he could deliver.

Shane already had come to the realization that being different can be a positive. He decided to apply that wisdom to the pros. He saw few NBA players were willing—or able—to make a crisp bounce pass, rotate when a teammate blew a defensive assignment, or give up their body to a big man charging through the lane.

Shane began to make those underappreciated parts of the game his specialty. He became a player who made his teammates better, with an extra pass, defensive help, and more. Before long, Shane was so good on defense that coaches routinely asked him to guard the league's best players, both guards and forwards— LeBron James, Chris Paul, Paul Pierce, and Carmelo Anthony.

A big part of why Shane embraced this unique game: He didn't care if he didn't look like the best athlete on the court, he says. That all stemmed from how comfortable Shane had become with himself.

"I had a willingness to take risks and look stupid,"

he says. "I don't know if I'd be where I am without [my unique experiences and background]."

His unique game also reflected Shane's intelligence and determination to study the game and discover advantages he had over rivals.

Here's an example of how Shane took a different approach to the NBA game. When most players backpedal on defense to try to stop a dribbler on a fast break, they usually jump as high as possible, with one goal in mind: blocking the shot. Swatting a ball away is among the flashiest defensive moves in basketball, especially when the offensive player is on the break with a head of steam. Blocked shots can be an instant momentum changer and highlight for that night's ESPN play-of-the-day countdown.

The problem is most defenders usually come up empty because it's very hard to stop someone barreling down the lane, flying sky-high to the basket. Contesting a shot usually results in a basket, and often leads to a foul as well, giving the offensive player a perfect chance for a three-point play.

Shane didn't want to give up a layup or a dunk if he could do something about it. He certainly didn't want to offer up a three-point play opportunity. And Shane didn't care about making *SportsCenter*.

That's why he embraced a different strategy. When a player like Kobe Bryant went up with the ball, Shane would pretend to jump with him to swat the ball away. But instead of raising his arms high to block the shot, Shane would stay low and swipe at the ball before it was raised up, knocking it out of the player's hands.

Shane's move often surprised opponents, resulting in steals or jump balls. That's because driving players usually focus on the rim on their way up—not on protecting the basketball. They're vulnerable as they soar higher, Shane realized. He took advantage by stripping the ball when rivals least expected it.

This is how Shane explained his distinctive defensive strategy to a reporter: "I know I can't really jump with a guy like Danny Granger. I'm not gonna meet him at the rim or make a play at the rim on LeBron [James] or Dwyane [Wade]. But I know my strength is that I have pretty good hand-eye coordination, so I try to get the ball as they're bringing it up early."

Shane's defensive strategies worked on most opponents. But not Kobe Bryant, the great Lakers shooting guard. As a rookie, Bryant lit up Shane and his teammates, dropping fifty-six points in just three quarters in one game. Bryant didn't even have to play in the fourth quarter because the Lakers were winning by such a large margin.

Getting schooled by Bryant ticked Shane off. "I was upset," he says. "No one wants to be torched, but I vowed never to let that happen again."

After an embarrassing string of failures, Shane began studying Bryant's game, watching hours of video, looking for any weaknesses. Bryant is one of the greatest players in NBA history and has few flaws. But even the best players have spots on the court where they feel less comfortable shooting, Shane knew. He made it his goal to force Bryant into those spots.

"That was my life; I studied everything about him, his tendencies and weaknesses," Shane says. "By the end, I knew Kobe better than he knew himself."

In 2006, after Shane was traded to the Houston Rockets, he regularly matched up against Bryant in Western Conference games. Shane found more success slowing Bryant down. Bryant still scored twenty points on most nights, but the points usually came with a poor field goal percentage and a Lakers loss, which was exactly what Shane hoped to achieve.

One way Shane used to keep Bryant in check was by putting a hand in Bryant's face as he shot. It was the kind of savvy strategy that older guys employ at local YMCAs when they try to slow down younger and more talented opponents. In the NBA, however, defenders usually go for steals and blocks, but few spend much energy putting hands in offensive players' faces. It was one more example of how Shane made himself into a player who refused to be concerned about looking bad.

"Someone [put a hand in] my face once and I hated it, so I knew if I hated it, my opponent would hate it," Shane says. "People get so caught up in 'looking cool' when playing sports, but I never worried about that. The hand in the face worked—even if Kobe wouldn't admit it!"

Shane used the same strategy against many of the league's top shooting guards. There's nothing wrong with blocking the vision of a shooter. But it makes a defender pretty unpopular. Stars like Bryant get annoyed, and it leads to a lot of trash talk. Also, a hand in the face of a shooter can sometimes lead to a foul. But Shane had better hand-eye coordination than most and knew just when to put his hand in a shooter's face without leading to contact and a foul.

"It's not illegal, but people like Kobe hated it," Shane says. "I didn't care what I looked like, though. I knew it affected their vision and shooting; that was my trick."

One game in 2008, Bryant came into Houston for a nationally televised game determined to light up Shane and the Rockets. Shane knew he would have his hands full. Bryant was stubborn; he wanted to prove the hand Shane put in his face wouldn't affect his shooting.

"He was super aggressive, he kept going to the shot, he threw the entire kitchen sink at me and scored twenty-six points," Shane says. "But he shot eleven for thirty-three, the second-most missed shots in his career. It was my proudest moment as a defender." The Lakers lost the game.

Shane made a career out of doing the little things on the court that were appreciated by coaches and teammates, even if his contributions didn't always receive the acclaim of fans, count for much in box scores, or make highlight reels. If Shane couldn't grab a rebound, sometimes he'd tip the ball to a teammate. On defense, he would leave his man to block out the opponent's best rebounder. Once, Shane asked his coach to come off the bench with the backups, rather than start, just so he could guard Manu Ginobili, the sweet-scoring sixth man for the San Antonio Spurs who had been scoring at will against the Rockets.

The Rockets' general manager, Daryl Morey, couldn't believe it when Shane made his request. "No one in the NBA does that," he told a writer. "No one says, 'Put me on the bench so I can guard their best scorer.'"

This is what Shane meant by not caring how he looked or what others thought. He learned to develop and appreciate his own style, and it made him a player most coaches wanted on their team. His unique style of play didn't always look the coolest, but it helped his team win. Indeed, in 2012 and 2013, Shane won NBA Championships while playing with LeBron James and the Miami Heat.

When he meets kids today, Shane shares lessons from his own experiences, which he says can be relevant to every kind of kid, not just those who grow up in a mixed-race household or those dealing with challenges on the court.

"When I was eight, nine, or ten, I wish I could have seen a snapshot of myself at thirty-five or thirty-six and how awesome it is to be different and not like everyone else," he says. "It's not just okay; it's awesome; that's what makes life fun—being different and creating your own path and flavor in sports, school, or family.

"Life is an adventure. I wouldn't trade my journey and struggles for anything in the world. It makes me appreciate everyone, their strengths and weaknesses, and adds so much flavor to life," Shane says. "Be proud of your heritage and who you are."

R.A. DICKEY

R.A. Dickey hit rock bottom in late September 2006.

Robert Allen Dickey's early life had been difficult and his parents usually weren't around. During his childhood, R.A. was forced on multiple occasions to endure the horrors of sexual abuse, leaving him overcome with shame. Sports became a salvation and R.A., as everyone called him, thrived on the baseball field. His talent led R.A. to the major leagues in 1996 when he was selected in the first round of the MLB Draft by the Texas Rangers. But just before he could sign a million-dollar contract, the team discovered R.A. didn't have a key ligament in his throwing arm and quickly withdrew its offer.

R.A. persevered, but in late 2006, he hit a brick

wall. R.A. endured a minor league season in which he gave up nearly five runs a game; his numbers were so awful that his future was in serious jeopardy. He had a growing family and was dealing with serious financial pressures. Desperate to end the pain, R.A. sat alone in his car on an empty Nashville street, weighing the best way to end his life.

This is it, R.A. recalls thinking.

R.A.'s challenges began early in life. His parents, both star local athletes, married at a young age, his mother just nineteen and father twenty-two. Money was tight and the marriage soon failed. After the divorce, R.A. lived with his mother, Leslie, who was loving and nurturing. She soon began spending much of her time at a local bar called Joe's Village Inn, however, drinking Miller Lite beers with friends as R.A. played video games elsewhere in the bar.

Empty beer cans piled up in their home garbage as Leslie increasingly turned to alcohol for comfort. She juggled several jobs and sometimes fell asleep as soon as she got home from work, leaving R.A. to fend for himself.

"She had an addiction, and over the years it got worse," R.A. says. "By the time I started going to middle school, she had a pretty significant problem."

R.A.'s other family members were battling their own demons. One Christmas, R.A. watched his uncle Ricky slap R.A.'s grandfather hard across the face, knocking him against the oven, after a round of heavy drinking. Watching his loved ones pound each other, R.A. turned sad, vowing never to touch alcohol.

Soon, his life became more turbulent. One hot July evening in 1983, when R.A. was eight years old, his mother said she was going out for the evening and that a new babysitter would be watching R.A. and his sister. His mother and her friends fixed drinks before heading out, giggling and laughing, paying little attention to what was going on elsewhere in the home. Left alone, the babysitter, a thirteen-year-old tall and athletic girl, took R.A. by the hand and led him to an upstairs bedroom. The girl's grip was firm, and she was insistent.

Upstairs, the babysitter told R.A. to remove his clothing. Sweating from every pore, R.A. thought about screaming for help or running away, but he felt compelled to follow her orders. She was older and R.A. felt defenseless. Before he realized what had happened, she had violated R.A., leaving him shaken and confused.

What actually had happened? Why had she touched him like that? Had he done something wrong?

"At eight, you don't know the difference between playing doctor and someone taking advantage of you," R.A. says. "But there was something about it that didn't feel right at all."

The babysitter violated R.A. four or five more times that summer, making him promise not to tell anyone what had happened. R.A. was left with a sense of guilt, as if he had done something improper.

"I felt a lot of shame, so I didn't tell anyone," he says. "That brought feelings of loneliness."

Two months later, after R.A started fourth grade, he and his mother and sister drove to the country-side outside Nashville to visit family. While R.A. was throwing a tennis ball off the roof of a nearby garage, a tall boy, who looked about sixteen or seventeen, approached. Before R.A. could say anything, the boy had unzipped his pants. R.A. tried to run, but the kid grabbed him, sexually assaulting R.A. The event traumatized R.A. for years to come.

"The second time was worse," R.A. says. "Instinctively, there was something about it that felt abnormal to me, and it was much more forceful."

As his family drove home, R.A. was sad and embarrassed. He climbed into bed, pulled the covers over his head, and prayed.

R.A. became more guarded, unwilling to open up with friends or family. The shame of the experiences was so overwhelming that it silenced R.A., leaving him to cope with the pain and guilt on his own.

"It made me someone who couldn't trust others," he says. "It happened so early in my life that it stunted my growth as a human being and didn't allow for a relationship. . . . I started to develop a chip on my shoulder."

Soon, R.A. found himself in fistfights. In school, on the playground, on the football field, and elsewhere. Some of it was just growing up and becoming "a low-level troublemaker," as R.A. describes it. But it was hard not to make the connection to the unsettling events that still weighed on the boy.

R.A. felt alone, but his experience was more common than he realized at the time. One male in six will be sexually abused before the age of eighteen, according to some estimates. Approximately 70 percent of the time, the abuse is by someone trusted and close to the family, the data says, something that can make it harder for a young person to view perpetrators in a bad light—and easier to blame themselves for the abuse.

"In my mind, I had it messed up; I thought I'd done something wrong, I had brought the abuse on myself, somehow; I had a part in it," R.A. says. "There's a lot of guilt and shame; shame is the most potent of feelings."

R.A.'s parents didn't talk very much, but they could sense that something was wrong and knew R.A. had to change his life. When he turned thirteen, R.A. got a lucky break—his parents helped him gain admission to the Montgomery Bell Academy (MBA), a prestigious all-boys school in Nashville known for its discipline, athletics, and strong academics. R.A.'s parents didn't have the money to pay the school's tuition, but MBA offered a full package of financial aid. R.A. hadn't performed well enough in the classroom to prove he could handle the rigor of the school, but he managed to pass an entrance test and MBA said he could enroll as long as he repeated seventh grade.

Getting into MBA was a lucky break, but at home, R.A.'s life was deteriorating. R.A.'s mother was becoming an outright alcoholic, graduating from beer to vodka. Meanwhile, R.A was turning into a "completely self-involved teenage punk," he recalls in his book *Wherever I Wind Up*. He battled his mother over almost every request she made, and turned unruly and obnoxious.

Before starting at MBA, R.A. stuffed some clothing into a duffel bag and left home to live with his father, hoping to spark a connection with him. R.A. left without even giving a hug good-bye to his sobbing mother, who was angry at herself for the destructive decisions she'd made in her life and how her relationship with R.A. had deteriorated.

"What's wrong with living here?" she asked him on his way out, almost pleading.

Nothing, R.A. responded. He just wanted to live with his father.

But it didn't take long before R.A.'s hopes of forging a connection with his father were dashed. His father quickly turned distant. When R.A. came home late, his father didn't even bother to ask where he had been. R.A. waited in vain for a hug or some sign of encouragement.

One day during his junior year in high school, after leaving his friend's house, R.A. decided he no longer could bear living in his father's home. Driving around town, he saw a house for rent. There was no alarm, dog, or furniture visible; R.A. lifted a plant pot up and found a key. He knew it was against the law and was scared he might get caught, but R.A. turned the key and tiptoed into complete darkness. Brushing away a few dead bugs, R.A. laid some towels in the corner of a bare living room, placed sweatshirts underneath him, and fell asleep.

The first night was a bit scary. But soon, R.A. became more comfortable sneaking into homes in the pitch dark and more adept at discovering ways to get in. R.A. slept in vacant houses a half dozen times over the next few years. He developed a clever strategy to ease the process. Sometimes he'd go to the library and read newspaper listings to find homes near school that were available, storing a sleeping bag in his car to make relocating easier.

He was lonely, but it was "a loneliness of my choosing," according to R.A, making him feel a bit better.

His new school began to have a positive impact on his self-esteem. An English teacher told R.A. he had an original mind, boosting his confidence. Around that time, he discovered he loved to read. And R.A. became closer with a friend named Bo Bartholomew, who had a cute, blond younger sister named Anne, an added reason for R.A. to make repeated visits to the Bartholomew home.

Bo introduced R.A. to church. R.A. didn't know much about religion, but he gained a sense of comfort turning to God.

"I had always thought I had to be this all-American boy to have people appreciate who I was," R.A. says. "But there were all these great stories in the New and Old Testament; God really cared for people who were broken and didn't necessarily have everything together."

There was somewhere else R.A. felt comfortable: the ball field. His arm had always been strong, making him an ideal pitching candidate. But there was something else that appealed to a boy dealing with a chaotic life.

"I trust baseball and I trust football and basketball," R.A. wrote in his book. "I trust my ability to play them and I trust that the games and completion will follow a prescribed order, even if you don't know who's going to win . . . it insulat[ed] me from everything else: my mother's increasing alcohol problem and my father's increasing aloofness."

As R.A. became occupied with sports at school, he

found a much-needed distraction from the difficult aspects of his life.

"Sports became a real sanctuary, a place where I could escape the reality of my world," R.A. says. "I'd disappear into a world where I didn't have to worry."

During seventh grade, R.A began to gain notice for his athletic ability. In one game, he struck out twelve batters in six innings while pitching his team to a league championship. As an eighth grader, R.A. made the high school varsity team, which was a huge accomplishment at the ultra-competitive school.

"I felt I messed up away from the field, but on the field, I was the best out there," he says. "[Being chosen for the varsity team,] validated those feelings and gave me a feeling of arrogance."

During his sophomore year, big-league scouts came to see R.A. pitch. They saw something special in him and loved how hard he competed. At the end of his senior year of high school in 1993, R.A. was named Tennessee's Player of the Year. He received scholarship offers for basketball and football, but R.A.'s heart was in baseball, and he enrolled in the University of Tennessee as a top recruit.

At Tennessee, R.A. became the workhorse of the pitching staff, and was named an All-American as a hard-throwing righty. He thrived in the classroom, too, with a grade point average of 3.35. In his sophomore year, R.A. threw 183 pitches in a single game to give Tennessee its first spot in the College World Series in forty-four years. But he never felt comfortable opening up with teammates or others about the ordeals of his past. You can't get burned if you don't open up, R.A. figured.

"I would only share pieces of myself with people; I would never fully engage in a relationship," he says. "I've had a lot of success in my athletic career, but ninety percent of it has been almost sad because I haven't known how to share it with others or celebrate it."

R.A. started for Team USA in the 1996 Olympics and was drafted that same year by the Texas Rangers with the eighteenth pick in Major League Baseball's amateur draft, receiving a signing bonus of $810,000. R.A. made plans to buy Anne—Bo's sister—a beautiful engagement ring. After spending so many nights with a rolled-up towel for a pillow and sweatshirts for a mattress, R.A. prepared to enjoy all the comforts and successes life has to offer.

Around that time, Danny Wheat, the trainer for the Rangers, was walking through the clubhouse when he picked up a copy of *Baseball America* magazine with a photo of R.A. posing alongside other starters for Team USA. Something about R.A.'s arm looked odd to Wheat. It was hanging at a weird angle, he thought, as if he had an elbow problem of some kind.

The team decided to run some tests, but R.A. wasn't very worried. He'd never experienced any troubles and his fastball could hit ninety-five miles an hour. Surely the doctors would give him a clean bill of health.

A bit later, R.A. and his agent flew to Arlington, Texas, to meet Rangers general manager Doug Melvin and the team's doctor. He broke some shocking news: R.A.'s elbow was missing an ulnar collateral ligament, or UCL. The UCL is a stabilizing ligament that's usually indispensable to anyone throwing a baseball. Dr. James Andrews, a world-renowned Alabama specialist who had operated on thousands of pitchers, told R.A he'd never examined anyone without a UCL; R.A. shouldn't even be able to turn a doorknob or shake hands without intense pain, Dr. Andrews said. R.A. either had been born without a UCL or the tissue had somehow disintegrated years earlier, the doctor said.

The Rangers decided to retract the team's contract offer to R.A., Melvin said. The risk was just too high, he explained.

R.A. was crushed. In an instant, he had lost most

of his bonus money, and it wasn't clear if he would ever pitch in the majors. For years, R.A. had tried to cover up the pain of his youth with success on the mound. Now, being told something was wrong with him, despite all the accolades, R.A. felt the world was confirming something he himself had long suspected. R.A. was transported back to his painful childhood; once again, he felt different from others.

To R.A., the diagnosis and the decision by the Rangers to pull the contract were confirmation that he was a damaged person and never should have placed his trust in others.

"It opened up a wound; you start to feel broken all over again," R.A. says. "The confusion and shame came back, all the things I tried to cover up as an athletic superstar."

R.A. seethed, angry at the Rangers, God, and the world.

"Imagine winning the lottery and then losing the ticket," R.A. later told the *New York Times*.

Eventually, Melvin called R.A. He felt bad about breaking R.A.'s heart and offered a $75,000 contract to join the team. It was a pittance compared to his earlier offer, but R.A. accepted, sad but determined to show the team he could become a star, even without a UCL.

In the back of his mind, however, R.A. couldn't stop thinking about the team's reaction and their subsequent bonus offer. He knew it was made out of guilt, rather than a conviction in his pitching skills and future. For the first time, his abilities on the mound were being questioned. Once confident, R.A. turned insecure. Maybe the Rangers' doubts were well founded, he thought. Maybe he'd never succeed.

R.A. had some strong seasons in the minor leagues, but they usually weren't enough to warrant much interest by the Rangers. It took five long years, but in 2001, when R.A. was twenty-six years old, he finally got the call to join the major-league club. By then, R.A. was almost ancient in baseball years, but it didn't matter. He had made it to the majors, finally.

The early results were awful, however—he allowed six runs in just four and two-thirds innings—and R.A. was sent right back to the minors. The Rangers didn't think too much of R.A.'s stuff. Neither did R.A.

Over the next few years, R.A. toiled away in the minor leagues, sometimes excelling and often struggling. Money was tight for R.A's growing family. During the off-seasons, he sometimes worked in a physical therapy center, helping middle-aged businessmen with troublesome hamstrings and elderly women with aching shoulders. R.A. looked into getting a full-time job at a Nashville YMCA, worried his future wouldn't include baseball. After seven long years as a member of the Triple-A Oklahoma City RedHawks, some locals even suggested that he run for mayor.

For some reason, R.A. was losing his fastball. Each year at spring training, his go-to pitch was a few miles per hour slower. Without a fastball, R.A. was like a superhero stripped of his special power. Trying to get batters out, R.A. felt almost naked; he was scared each pitch would demonstrate how inadequate he was as a player and a person.

In the past, R.A. had relied on sports to build self-confidence. The approach worked well when he was dominating batters in high school and college. Now R.A. couldn't find a way to get anyone out and had nothing to fall back on.

"I realized I was living a life where my self-worth was tied up in being an athlete," he says.

Sometimes, as R.A. practiced in the bullpen, trying to locate his missing fastball and adjust to his limited arsenal of pitches, he played around with throwing a knuckleball, a pitch his grandfather had taught him.

"I always had a pretty good knuckleball; my grand-father had a good one and had showed me the grip," R.A. recalls.

One day during spring training in 2005, Rangers pitching coach Orel Hershiser, who had starred as a hurler on the Los Angeles Dodgers' starting pitching staff in his playing days, noticed R.A.'s knuckleball. A bit later, he called R.A. into the manager's officer, where Rangers manager Buck Showalter was waiting.

"Would you be willing to go back to the minors to learn to throw a knuckleball?" Showalter asked. He and Hershiser said it was R.A.'s best chance for suc-cess. They knew R.A. was a hard worker who might be able to master the pitch.

R.A. figured he didn't have much of a choice. "By 'willing,' they meant if you don't do it we're probably going to release you," R.A. jokes.

Most important, R.A. was tired of being a mediocre major-league pitcher and welcomed an opportunity to improve his game before it was too late. He was thirty-one years old and had two young daughters. A baby boy on the way. To save money, he had begun riding to the ballpark on a borrowed bicycle.

There were other reasons the knuckleball felt right to R.A.

"Organizations don't want the pitch around, it's too unpredictable, they think the other shoe will drop," R.A. says. "It's a very lonely pitch"—a feeling R.A. was familiar with.

Baseball historians trace the knuckleball—which aims to minimize the ball's spin, allowing it to make erratic changes in direction—back to the early twentieth century. But few in high school, college, or the pros throw the pitch. Just a handful of pitchers built Hall of Fame careers relying on it, including Hoyt Wilhelm and Phil Niekro.

For one thing, it's almost impossible to master. It sometimes takes a pitcher years to dig his nails into the baseball the right way and figure out the proper grip and mechanics. Also, it's a pitch that commands little respect from most managers and players, mostly because it's painfully slow, usually coming in at around seventy miles an hour. Many coaches view it as a bit of a circus pitch, capable of getting a few batters out and entertaining fans, yet too unpredictable to rely on.

Coaches usually can't even help a knuckleballer improve his delivery and accuracy since they have such little understanding of the pitch.

"People fear what they don't understand," R.A. says.

But R.A. knew his fastball had disappeared and he needed to find a way to succeed in the majors, so he embraced the idea. It was tough, though. Knuckleballs have to be thrown slowly, something former fireballers like R.A. aren't accustomed to doing. His own minor-league pitching coaches had no clue how to teach the pitch, so R.A. was on his own.

In April 2006, R.A. took the mound for the Rangers against the Detroit Tigers. In the bullpen, his knuckleball was working well, and R.A. was hopeful. Just two pitches into the game, though, leadoff hitter Brandon Inge drove a pitch deep and over the left field fence. Later that inning, Tigers slugger Magglio Ordóñez ripped another knuckleball over that same wall.

R.A. looked over at first basemen Mark Teixeira and the rest of his teammates and felt awful, like he was letting everyone down. Before the fourth inning was over, R.A. had allowed seven runs, including six home runs, tied for the most given up by any starting pitcher since 1900.

After the game, R.A.'s manager struggled to find something to say to keep R.A.'s spirits up.

"If you look for positives, some of the homers were solos," Buck Showalter told reporters. "But I'm really reaching."

R.A. was harder on himself. He felt his self-confidence evaporating.

What have I done? R.A. asked himself.

"I had no one to lean on," he recalls.

After his pitiful performances, R.A. was sent back down to the minors and finished the 2006 season with the Triple-A Oklahoma City RedHawks. He racked up an embarrassing ERA of 4.92. In other words, on average, he gave up nearly five runs for every nine innings he pitched. R.A. didn't seem to have any hope of turning things around. He began to spiral, his feelings of guilt and shame rushing back.

"I wish I would have just been open and transparent about what was going on with people who wanted to sit with my pain," R.A. says.

One morning, R.A. awoke on his couch feeling a darkness he never before had experienced. He felt boxed in, with no possible means of escape. He began to contemplate ending it all, perhaps by revving his car's engine in his garage and suffering carbon monoxide poisoning.

"I was sitting in my car, contemplating suicide; I knew if I turned a key, that would be it," he says.

R.A. began to think about his children. Slowly, he regained his resolve to live. He was proud of how hard he always fought on the mound, even when he didn't have his best stuff. R.A. made a promise to fight just as hard in life, too.

"I chose hope," R.A. says.

He agreed to work with a therapist a friend had recommended months earlier. R.A. knew he had no choice but to open up and be honest about his past. The very next day, he began speaking with the therapist.

R.A. began to learn about himself and confront his difficult childhood—his poverty, the difficult relations with his family, the sexual abuse, and his years of hiding his secret. R.A. learned to trust his therapist and confront his demons.

"I needed to know what it was like to risk trusting others," he recalls, something he says therapy helped him discover.

It's likely no coincidence that around the same time, R.A. began to figure out the knuckleball. Some of the progress came from digesting lessons from former pitchers who had mastered the pitch. Charlie Hough taught R.A. to move his nails until they were just underneath the horseshoe of the ball, resulting in a different and more effective grip. He also showed R.A.

how to keep his body from flying open when he threw the ball, reducing the ball's spin and allowing it to dart at the last second. Phil Niekro demonstrated how R.A. could bring his hips forward to give his pitches more energy and movement. Soon, the ball was dropping a foot just as it reached the plate.

In the spring of 2009, R.A. began seeing signs that he finally was in command of his knuckleball. That spring, pitching for the Minnesota Twins, R.A. threw three knuckleballs to Baltimore Orioles leadoff hitter Brian Roberts. Roberts missed all three, the last one so badly his bat flew into the stands as R.A's catcher giggled. Back in the minors when the regular season began, R.A. started one game, giving up a leadoff blooper that fell for a hit. Then he retired twenty-seven straight batters, astounding himself and his teammates.

I got it. It's ready, R.A. thought.

"I had never felt like I had mastered it before; if I got someone out, I felt I was lucky," he says.

Reaching the majors again, R.A. struck out Milwaukee Brewers slugger Prince Fielder, who shook his head and muttered something under his breath that R.A could read from the mound:

"I can't believe he just did that!" Fielder exclaimed.

"Guys like [outfielder] Adam Jones who are more

animated in the box would say things," as they struck out, R.A. says. "My catcher would come back and say things like 'How do you ever give up a hit?' It was a great feeling."

R.A. became a star pitching for the New York Mets in 2010 when he recorded an ERA of 2.84 and eleven victories. The Mets showed so much confidence in R.A. that they signed him to a two-year contract worth $7.8 million. Finally, R.A. had achieved financial security.

In 2012, R.A. was selected to his first All-Star Game. That year, he set a Mets franchise record by pitching thirty-two and two-thirds consecutive scoreless innings and won the National League Cy Young Award for the best pitcher, becoming the first knuckleballer to win the prestigious award.

When the rebuilding Mets decided to trade R.A. for a group of blue-chip prospects, the Toronto Blue Jays eagerly agreed to a deal. By the summer of 2015, R.A. was heading the pitching rotation as the first-place Blue Jays headed into the play-offs.

In the American League division series, R.A. faced the Texas Rangers, the very team that had drafted him and let him go at the start of his career. Starting his first play-off game in his career, a forty-year-old R.A. didn't seem nervous, even though he was pitching in a hostile Texas ballpark. Instead, he reflected on the unlikely arc of his career.

"It's poetic, that's what it is for me," R.A. told reporters. "It's a neat narrative."

That day, R.A. held the Rangers to just one run in a Blue Jays victory.

Earlier that summer, sitting in the dugout before a big showdown in New York against the Yankees, R.A. spoke about how he'd managed to reclaim his career.

"Now I know my [pitching] mechanics well enough that I know the results will be there," he says. The key to turning things around, he said, was sharing his pain and being honest about his past. R.A. urges young people to open up about their issues.

"Be honest about what hurts you, even if it's difficult and you think no one will understand," he says. "If your life has been broken, there's still usually one person you can open up to, maybe a hotline or a therapy center. Try to find one person so you don't feel so alone. People are there for you.

"My biggest piece of advice is to risk being honest about your story," R.A. says. "People care."

SERGE
IBAKA

Poverty. Wartime violence. The loss of his mother and arrest of his father.

Serge Ibaka would have to overcome those imposing obstacles if he wanted to become a basketball superstar.

Born in September 1989, Serge grew up in Brazzaville, the capital of the Republic of the Congo, a poor African nation plagued by a history of warfare. Early on, Serge seemed to have clear advantages over most of his friends. Serge's mother, Amadou Djonga, came from a middle-class family that was more comfortable financially than many others in Brazzaville.

"She had money, and she gave me a PlayStation and other good things," Serge says. "We were very close."

Amadou, a former member of her country's women's basketball team, loved her son and brought him to church each week, forging a close bond. She had big plans for Serge and was determined to give him a top-notch education outside the country.

When Serge was just seven years old, though, Amadou became sick. Serge didn't know what was wrong with his mother and family members wouldn't share any details of the illness, as if they were hiding a secret they didn't think the boy could handle.

One day after school, as Serge prepared to leave with his friends, he was asked to stay behind to speak with a school official. A little while later, the official arrived to share some shocking news: Serge's mother had died.

Unable to comprehend the news, Serge collapsed to the ground.

"I knew she was sick, but I didn't think she was that sick," he recalls.

For weeks, Serge was in a state of shock, displaying few emotions, unable even to cry. Most days, he couldn't even get out of bed. Losing a mother is always a harsh blow, but the sudden news made it even more difficult to handle. Serge was told his mother had died of natural causes, making the tragedy even more baffling. To this day, he still doesn't know what caused his mother's untimely death.

"I was so dependent on my mother; her death was just something I never thought could happen," he says. "It changed everything."

After a period of confusion, Serge began to cry. He bawled all the time, out of the blue, often for no reason. For months, crying was about all he managed to do.

Everything reminded Serge of his mother. Even when he went to visit his grandmother, Christine Djonga, a loving woman who in the past always put a smile on Serge's face, he couldn't shake the sadness. Before she passed away, Serge's mother had joined him on these visits. Now, with her gone, the experience of seeing his grandmother brought up fresh memories of those good times.

"Every time I visited my grandmother, I started crying, I was so sad," he says. "It was hard, really hard; it was depressing."

Without his mother to lend financial and emotional support, Serge's hopes of leaving the country to get an education were dashed and he became discouraged about his future.

"My dream of going to Europe for school was ruined," says Serge, who would remain stunned by the death many years later. "I lost all my passion."

Serge began to spend much more time with his father, Désiré Ibaka. He had played basketball professionally in Africa and for the national team of the Republic of the Congo but was poorer than Serge's mother's family and wasn't living with her at the time of her death.

Searching for a distraction, Serge turned to basketball, a sport both his parents had loved. Serge began heading to local courts to join pickup games with other young people, discovering he enjoyed the game. Serge started playing every day, sometimes for six hours straight. The practice and dedication paid off—Serge soon was better than many of the older kids in the neighborhood.

"Basketball was an escape; it helped me not think about what I didn't have," Serge says. "If I didn't play for a day, I felt really bad."

Basketball also may have been a way for Serge to maintain a connection with his mother and her memory. Indeed, neighbors and family members reminded Serge that both his parents had played ball professionally. They encouraged him to keep at it, saying he might have a future in the sport.

"It was my dad's dream for me to play basketball," Serge says. "I wore his jersey number, number nine."

Just as Serge was settling into a new routine, civil

unrest broke out in Brazzaville and elsewhere in the country. Fighting between ethnic groups over the nation's vast oil reserves led to the largest war in modern African history, a battle that included eight different nations and a death toll of more than five million.

Searching for safety, Serge and his family fled north, settling in a river town of twenty-five thousand people called Ouésso that's surrounded by a rain forest. Once, he had video games, movies, and the prospect of a top education. Now Serge, just nine years old, lived in a series of ramshackle homes without any electricity or running water. His life wasn't easy before; now it had become much more difficult.

"We heard bombs every second, every minute," he says. "We called it music because we heard it all the time, all day, twenty-four hours, no stop."

Fighting continued for the next few years as Serge and his family did their best to stay out of danger. They remained safe, but Serge was nervous much of the time, forced to witness wartime horrors.

"People got killed right in front of me; it was crazy to see someone die," he says. "I heard fighting in the streets a lot; I was very scared."

Serge began to see the personalities of young people around him change, even those not involved in the fighting. Friends resorted to violence, usually with little justification.

"In war, everyone has guns. The mentality is to act tough; everyone thinks they're tough," he says. "Friends killed each other for five dollars."

The violence and surprising death of his mother taught Serge some powerful early lessons about the brutalities of life and how wealth provides limited protection against tragedy.

"I learned that everyone dies all the same; they all looked the same when they died [both rich and poor]," he says. "You don't have anything when you die."

Serge and his family returned home to Brazzaville in 2002, when Serge was thirteen, but the nation was still dealing with heated political conflict. His father, Désiré, needed to find work to help provide for Serge and his other children. So Désiré went back to his old job at a port a few miles away, just across the border, in the neighboring country of the Democratic Republic of the Congo.

One day, Désiré was grabbed and thrown in jail, accused of being disloyal to the government simply because he had crossed the border for his job.

Serge already had lost his mother. Now his father had been taken away as a political prisoner. Adding to his anguish: For months, Serge didn't even know what had happened to his father. He had disappeared, and no one was sure where he was until word emerged that he was sitting in prison.

"It was so stressful," Serge says.

For two years, Serge didn't go to school because he had no one to pay the required fees. Often, he had no one to take care of him.

Eventually, Serge went to live with his grandmother, who at that point was trying to raise more than a dozen of Serge's siblings. There was always someone at home. But in many ways, Serge had never felt so alone. He missed his parents and had no one he could turn to when he wanted to share his anxieties.

"There were twenty people in the house; my grandmother really had no time for me," he says. "It was just a place for me to sleep. I was really on my own."

Serge was sad and worried all the time. One day, Serge decided he'd had enough of feeling down and depressed. He began thinking about how to make something of his life.

"I said I'm going to fight, I'm going to find a better way, a better life for myself," he says.

Serge started to focus on the one thing that gave him pleasure: basketball.

"I didn't have vacations, video games, or anything," Serge says. "Basketball was the only way for me to enjoy life."

Soon, Serge was dreaming of playing basketball professionally in his country or somewhere else in Africa. After school each day, Serge headed to nearby courts that had wooden backboards and bent rims. Serge didn't mind the poor condition of the courts; they were all he knew, and he was enjoying the competition too much to complain. All weekend long he continued working on his game.

"Basketball took away all the stress," he says. "I could be hungry, but I'd go and play ball for six hours and forget it all."

Serge's father remained in prison for nearly two years. Slowly, with his father still in jail, Serge began to appreciate living in a home with so many relatives. Serge became closer with his grandmother. And living with so many brothers and sisters for the first time began to help alleviate some of the boy's sadness.

"It felt good. They were like my friends," Serge says. "I liked growing up in a family atmosphere. . . . Family is very important in Africa."

Serge and his friends didn't have money for new basketball gear. Many local kids played in plastic shoes, but Serge was lucky to have a pair of old sneakers. They were flimsy, though, and it got so hot some days that Serge's sneakers began to melt on the cracked, scalding-hot concrete court. Soon, holes formed in his shoes, and it was hard to play ball. His friends were dealing with the same issues with their own sneakers.

Serge could only afford one pair of nice shoes, which he wore to school, so new sneakers were out of the question. Serge and his friends didn't want to give up basketball, though, so they developed a creative way to deal with the oppressive heat.

"I lost so many shoes that I began just using old ones and reinforcing them with cardboard," he says. The cardboard helped to cover up the holes in his shoes.

Serge didn't resent the hardships—he tried to adjust to them, relying in part on his religious upbringing.

"I didn't have Nintendos or iPods, but I was happy," he says. "In life that's how it is, that's how God created us. Some have less, some have more. I had food, friends, and a place to sleep—that's all I needed."

Serge practiced on the court whenever he could, hoping one day to become a professional basketball player. He sometimes got up at 4:00 a.m. to run, trying to improve his conditioning.

"I was dreaming, I was believing, I was working," he told the online publication Grantland.

Friends laughed when Serge shared his dream. Look at your father, they said. He also wanted to make a career of playing basketball, but he ended up in prison, they reminded him.

"You're not going to make it," a friend cautioned Serge one day.

Even family members advised Serge to stop wasting so much time playing ball. Get a stable army job like your friends, they advised him.

Serge did his best to ignore the doubters, though part of him wondered if he was making a mistake.

"I also thought maybe I should just go to the army. I needed money; it was hard," he says. "I stood up to them, but it was hard, like a fight."

On Saturday nights, when his friends put on their best clothes, took any money they had saved, and went to a popular local dance club, Serge remained on the court, practicing his shooting and rebounding, hoping the endless hours on the court would pay off someday.

Some kids teased Serge when he wouldn't come with them to party. "You don't have any money or nice clothes?" one boy said. "Or you just can't get a girl?"

"Guys made jokes about me," says Serge. "I chose to sacrifice the moment because it's just a short moment. . . . I knew that club wasn't going anywhere."

A local coach named Maxim Mbochi who specialized in developing young players urged Serge to work hard on his game if he wanted to be a pro. Serge decided partying with his friends was a distraction he couldn't afford.

"You have to choose one life or another," Serge says. "On weekends, I couldn't do what everyone else was doing, but I knew my moment would come."

Serge enjoyed a rare understanding of the game, helped by the tutelage of his father, a six-foot-seven post player who had owned the paint when he played, gobbling up rebounds and blocking shots.

It soon became apparent that Serge, who was approaching seven feet, had the potential to be much better than his father. Even as a teenager, Serge had a low-post game few could match. He also had impressive shooting range for a big man. And his unusual agility and natural athleticism made it nearly impossible for opponents to contend with his game.

By the age of sixteen, coaches began coming to Serge's games to watch him play. That year, he was asked to join the country's under-eighteen team, an honor that reaffirmed Serge's decision to focus on basketball.

"This was my dream," Serge says. "It was proof that I was one of the best. I felt really special."

Serge got his first big test in 2006 when he and his team were invited to play in a tournament in Durban, South Africa. Serge knew scouts from all over Africa would be there. Perhaps he'd be able to impress someone who might help him achieve his goal of a pro career, he thought.

"It was the happiest moment of my life when I found out we were going," he says. "It felt like my dreams were coming true—this was my first big competition."

Serge's joy didn't last very long. He boarded the flight, buckled up, and took off for South Africa with his teammates. Then the plane began to shake.

Serge had never been on a plane before and didn't realize they can rock violently when there's turbulence. His coach told him that everything was fine, but Serge wasn't reassured.

He opened the window shade, saw how high in the air they were, and turned pale with panic. Serge started praying and sweating profusely, almost passing out.

"It was four hours of shaking, I felt like I was going to die," he says. "I didn't know it was normal!"

The airplane landed with a violent jolt, compounding Serge's anxiety. Getting off the plane, he swore he would never take another flight.

"The landing was the worst; I was shaking," he says. "I started to think I should have stayed home."

One good thing came from the stressful flight: The basketball tournament seemed a breeze by comparison. Serge competed against older, more experienced players, but he dominated almost every game. He scored more points, grabbed more rebounds, and had more blocked shots than anyone else and was voted the tournament's most valuable player. It was clear to everyone watching that Serge was a special talent.

"That's when people knew," he says.

In the stands, a scout working for international agent Pere Gallego took special interest in Serge. Gallego searched the world for young players with pro potential. Watching Serge score, rebound, and run, the scout loved what he saw.

"It was like a professional playing against kids," Gallego says.

A few weeks after the game, Gallego and his associates approached Serge. They knew Serge had the talent to be a pro but wanted to know if he had the hunger to get to the next level.

"After talking to him, his mind and focus [stood out]. . . . He was a hard worker and ready to sacrifice to achieve his dreams," Gallego says. "I've been in twelve African countries, scouting hundreds of players, and never have seen anybody like him. . . . He was a fighter, a winner, a leader."

A bit later, Gallego's agency contacted Serge's father to make a pitch—the agency could help Serge develop into a pro. But there was a catch—he'd have to move to Europe, where Gallego and his agency were based.

The flight to South Africa had been a nightmare. Serge dreaded the idea of doing any more flying. He also was wary of leaving his native country. The tumult in his life made him appreciate being around family members.

But playing pro basketball was his dream. Serge and his father knew this kind of opportunity might not come again, so they signed with Gallego. At the age of seventeen, Serge left the Republic of the Congo for France, and soon went on to Spain, where he was signed by a professional team.

Serge only spoke French and Lingala, the language

of his country. And he didn't know anyone in Spain, so he knew the transition would be difficult. But he was determined to try his best to become a pro basketball player.

Arriving in Spain, Serge forced himself to learn Spanish, read local sports publications, and get to know the nation's culture. In Barcelona, Serge lived with Jordi Ardèvol, the general manager of his first team, CB L'Hospitalet, who helped Serge adjust to life in Spain.

To relax at home and before games, Serge turned to the Bible, reading passages each day to calm himself.

"Little by little, I got used to everything," he says.

Scouts began saying that Serge might have a shot at playing in the NBA if he kept improving. During the summer of 2007, he was invited to an Adidas basketball camp in New Orleans, a showcase for players under the age of eighteen from all over the world.

When officials tested Serge's vertical jump, they were stunned. He jumped higher than the measuring device's pegs could even record. Soon, NBA scouts were buzzing about Serge's athleticism, energy, and potential. When they heard about the resilience and determination Serge displayed overcoming the challenges of growing up in the Congo, teams became even more impressed.

In the 2007–2008 season, playing with L'Hospitalet in Spain, Serge averaged 11.3 points and nearly 2 blocks per game, impressive numbers for a young man still learning to master the sport.

As the 2008 NBA Draft approached, some analysts said Serge had a shot at being picked in the first or second rounds. There were areas of his game he needed to work on, but Serge was a rare breed—big, athletic, and hungry to improve.

The night of the draft, Serge waited nervously to see if he would be chosen. Eighteen years old and wearing his very first suit, Serge shook with nerves as players came off the board and the first round got under way. The names of future stars were called as they were chosen: Derrick Rose, Russell Westbrook, Kevin Love, and more.

What happens if they don't pick me? Serge thought.

"It would be so embarrassing for me," he remembers. "I started praying, 'Can I hear my name?'"

Late in the first round, Serge's name finally was announced to the thousands of fans watching live from Madison Square Garden and at home on TV. The Oklahoma City Thunder had selected Serge with the twenty-fourth pick of the NBA Draft. It was the first time anyone from the Republic of the Congo ever had been drafted. He also was the youngest player drafted that year.

Serge breathed a huge sigh of relief.

Back home, Serge was an instant star, cheered by the proud citizens of his native country. Some friends still maintained doubts, though.

"They said, 'You'll play two or three years and then you'll be out of the league,'" Serge recalls.

Serge used the skepticism to fuel his daily workouts.

"It was a lesson for me; I wanted to keep getting better," he says.

Serge moved to Oklahoma City for the 2009–2010 season. Working with an English tutor who also cooked Congolese food, Serge learned to acclimate himself to life in America, just as he had in Spain, and continued turning to the Bible for support.

The hard work paid off. Within three years, Serge had established himself as one of the NBA's best big men. In the 2011–2012 season, Serge finished second in the Defensive Player of the Year voting behind New York Knicks center Tyson Chandler. In the 2012–13 season, Serge finished third in the voting and led the league in blocks for the second straight year. That year, Serge went eleven for eleven from the field in Game 4 of the Western Conference Finals against the San Antonio Spurs, helping to lead the Thunder past the Spurs to the 2012 NBA Finals, where they lost to LeBron James, Dwyane Wade, and the Miami Heat.

During the 2014–2015 season, Serge suffered from right knee soreness and eventually underwent surgery. If injuries hadn't slowed him, most analysts say he would have contended for the Defensive Player of the Year Award again that season. He began the 2015–2016 season among the league leaders in blocks and rebounds.

Even fierce opponents appreciate what Serge has endured to reach stardom.

"He's not one of the kids [who] at eighteen knew he was going to be a superstar, who was going to be a millionaire and take care of his family," says San Antonio Spurs shooting guard Manu Ginobili, a superstar himself. "When you hear stories like [Serge's] . . . you understand what adversity is. Adversity is not being 0–2 [in a play-off series]."

Today, many fans view Serge as having *made it*. He earns about $12 million a year and starts for a top NBA team. But Serge says he still feels pressure.

"The more you do, the more people expect," he says. "I have my contract, but I still have to sacrifice—I go to sleep early, eat well, take care of my body, and work to get better."

After the 2014 season, Serge flew back to Brazzaville to visit family. He and some friends went to a dance club—the same one Serge had passed on growing up so he could focus on basketball. This time, everyone in the club cheered their hometown hero, and the DJ boomed his name all night.

"That club didn't go anywhere after all," he says.

Serge advises young people to establish a goal, focus on it, and ignore distractions.

"All the pleasures of life will still be there later," he says. "For me to be in the NBA after everything that happened to me shows anything is possible if you really believe."

CARON BUTLER

aron Butler first became nervous when he saw federal agents roaming the halls of Racine Case High School, searching for someone.

Moments later, they burst into Caron's classroom, surrounding him. Within moments, Caron was under arrest. Agents of the Bureau of Alcohol, Tobacco, Firearms, and Explosives (ATF), had found drugs and a .32-caliber pistol in his locker. Soon, they discovered that Caron, a high school freshman, was carrying over a thousand dollars in cash, the obvious windfall of some serious drug dealing.

Caron grew up committing crimes in the streets of Racine, Wisconsin. That day, he had let someone store drugs and a gun in his locker. The police promised Caron a lighter sentence if he shared the name of the person who had placed the drugs and gun in the locker. Caron wouldn't cooperate, though, despite pleadings from his family.

Caron spent two months of an eighteen-month sentence at an adult facility called the Racine Correctional Institution. Then he was transferred to the Ethan Allen School for Boys, a campus for young people convicted of murder, burglary, drug dealing, and other serious crimes.

As Caron's prison bus made the one-hour trip to Ethan Allen, his mother drove in her station wagon, following the entire way. Caron cried as he saw his mother trailing behind. Just a few months earlier, Caron's uncle had been sentenced to ten months in prison on a gun charge. Now Caron's mother was horrified to watch her son being sent away, heading down the same destructive path.

At Ethan Allen, Caron was locked up with tough, angry young men, some who were even eighteen and nineteen years old. On the streets, Caron felt like a king, dealing cocaine and raking in thousands of dollars a week. In prison, Caron suddenly felt young and scared. Things soon would get much worse.

After getting into a fight with a fellow inmate who was a member of a rival gang, Caron was placed in solitary confinement. For fifteen days, he was alone "in the hole," confined to a small yellow brick cell with a steel bed and two-inch-thick mattress. No visitors were allowed and Caron didn't see a soul for twenty-three hours a day. His food was slid to him through a small opening in his cell door, and he was given just one hour each day to clean himself outside the cell.

"That was the hardest time I ever did," he told Fox Sports. "That was the moment I was broken."

Caron spent his time thinking about his life and writing emotional letters to his family about how blessed he was to have them and how much he had squandered by leading a life of crime and ending up in jail.

"I felt the failure of my grandmother looking at me. . . . That hurt bone deep," he says.

Caron realized he had let his family down; he cried as he pondered the many wrong turns of his young life.

I can't do this to my mother and grandmother. . . . My old ways ain't doing nothing for me, he remembers thinking.

Searching for inspiration, Caron sometimes read verses from a Bible his grandmother had sent him. Looking outside his cell's window, he saw a basketball court.

"God puts stuff in front of you for a reason," he

later told the *Washington Post*. "That was my ticket out."

Caron made a promise. When he got out of prison, he was going to turn his life around.

"I learned I have to have a will, have to be dedicated to what I wanted to do to be better," he said to Fox Sports.

Caron vowed to become the first male in the family to lead an upstanding life.

"It was a cycle of men in my family," he says. They broke the law, went to prison, got out, and got in trouble once again. "I wanted to break that cycle."

Escaping the hard life would be more difficult than Caron ever imagined.

Caron began dealing drugs at an early age. Growing up in a poor and violent area in the south side of Racine, Caron was raised by a single mother who juggled two jobs and sometimes worked eighty-hour weeks, which meant she couldn't always look after him. On his own, Caron would spend much of his time playing pickup basketball in a local community center or hanging out with friends at nearby Hamilton Park. But without constant adult supervision, he quickly found himself caught up in a life of crime.

When Caron was about ten years old, he began doing drug runs for local dealers. Sometimes he would sell drugs from a little red wagon. At twelve, he got up each morning around 3:00 a.m. for a local newspaper route. After he was done, he'd hit the corner, selling crack cocaine, often making over a thousand dollars in a single morning. At home, Caron would hide his gold watch and chains to avoid his mother's suspicion. Caron didn't try drugs himself, but his life revolved around selling them.

"Older members of my family introduced me to the [drug] game," Caron told Vice Media. "Sometimes, you go on your first bike ride and take the training wheels off; that's what your uncle did. . . . My uncle introduced me to the game, to hustling to pimping; that's what I was exposed to."

An epidemic of crack cocaine swept through the country in the 1990s, and drug dealing seemed both exciting and lucrative to Caron, who watched other kids in the neighborhood hauling garbage bags full of cash, the spoils of a life of crime. Young men looked up to the most successful dealers, who often were greeted like heroes on their return home from prison.

Caron witnessed the violence that came with the drug life, details of which he recounts in his book, *Tuff*

Juice. At twelve, Caron bought a .32 revolver for a hundred dollars. He and his friends would fire into Lake Michigan, scaring Jet Skiers and aiming at nearby boulders. Rival gang members wore masks during shoot-outs in a local park. Caron also saw the horrible effects drugs had on people he knew who were using. He remembers seeing his mother's boyfriend shooting heroin in their apartment. One day, Caron saw a mother in the neighborhood lying dead on the street in front of his home.

"I was always nervous, always scared, looking over my shoulder, thinking about being shot at," Caron told Fox Sports.

Caron hardly went to school. Instead, he and his friends got into trouble fighting and vandalizing property. Caron once estimated that he was arrested and sent to juvenile court fifteen times before the age of fifteen. At one point, a gang called the Gangster Disciples recruited Caron, telling him about the easy money he could make. His uncles and a few cousins already were in the business, so it was an easy pitch.

"I didn't see a guy dressing nice of my color, doing great things. That was all I knew," he says. "I was a lost kid."

Caron's arrest and the time he spent in solitary

confinement changed him, though. When he got out, he dedicated himself to staying on the right path and improving his basketball game. Hoping to make money in an honest way, Caron got a job at a Burger King restaurant five miles from his house, mopping floors, removing French fries from burning hot grease, and performing other menial jobs.

Friends came by to tease him for working at a restaurant.

"Friends clowned me. . . . They laughed at me, the uniform and everything," Caron recalls. "But I just stayed with it. . . . I had different plans. . . . I wanted to see how far my talents could take me."

After getting out of jail, Caron had to wear an electronic bracelet that monitored his whereabouts. Caron wore several pairs of socks to cover the bracelet, embarrassed about having to wear it. One time, when his ride home from the Burger King didn't show up, Caron sprinted for miles to get home, knowing he'd be sent back to prison if he violated his evening curfew.

"I just made it," he recalls.

His mother, Mattie Claybrook, was thrilled by the changes she was seeing in her son.

"I knew then he wasn't going to be in trouble anymore. . . . He had learned his lesson," she told Fox.

As Caron began to turn his life around, he started receiving some attention for his skills on the basketball court. Jameel Ghuari, the director of a local community center who coached Caron for an Amateur Athletic Union team, spent hours trying to convince Caron that he had so much talent that basketball could lead to a better life. But according to Ghuari, Caron hadn't completely shaken free from the pull of the street.

"He was still very influenced by his environment and those individuals who he hung around with," Ghuari says.

Soon, Caron was dominating all the best players in the state, including Tony Romo, the future Dallas Cowboys football star. At the age of seventeen, Caron's future seemed bright . . . until one January afternoon in 1998.

That's when the seventeen-year-old looked out the window of his home and saw sirens, commotion, and police. Officers were searching the area. Though Caron had been out of prison for a year and a half, he knew they'd be pounding on his door within moments. Caron was home sick that day with the flu; he got into bed, pulled the sheets over his head, and pretended to sleep.

Boom! Boom!

The officers, dressed in black, broke down the door

and stormed in, looking for evidence of drug dealing. Police had received a tip that there was drug activity in the garage of the home Caron shared with his mother and uncle. They didn't find anything in the home, but the police soon discovered 15.3 grams of cocaine in the garage.

The officers threw Caron on the couch and handcuffed him. Their case seemed solid. Caron was going to be sent away to prison once again, likely for at least ten years this time, given his prior arrests. His future seemed ruined.

Caron was in disbelief.

"I am *not* messing with dope right now," Caron insisted to the officers.

A young officer named Richard Geller, head of the department's investigations unit, was aware of Caron's past arrests. He didn't know he was a promising basketball player, but as he listened to Caron's protests, Geller began to believe he was innocent.

"He was a very scared kid," Geller recalls.

Geller called his commanders. They said there was enough evidence for an arrest, but he could let Caron go if he believed him. Geller said he did. He came back and uncuffed Caron.

"I hope I'm not making a mistake," Geller said.

That decision might've saved Caron's life.

Caron always had an interest in basketball. At Ethan Allen, he played pickup games to win Little Debbie snack cakes. Over time, as Caron decided to live a clean life, basketball became a passion.

In 1998, Caron played a tournament at Purdue University and won MVP honors, besting future NBA stars, including Dwyane Wade, Quentin Richardson, and Corey Maggette. Back home, Caron averaged twenty-four points and eleven rebounds a game during his junior year of high school, earning all-state honors.

But Caron realized he needed to leave Racine if he was going to make something of his life. One day, Caron borrowed five thousand dollars from a local drug dealer to pay the tuition at a prep school Ghuari had recommended, Maine Central Institute.

After two years in Maine, Caron caught the eye of Jim Calhoun, the legendary coach of the University of Connecticut basketball team. Calhoun was just as impressed with Caron's resilience and positive attitude as he was by his talent. Calhoun knew he wanted Caron on his team and offered the budding young talent a scholarship to attend the university.

At Connecticut, Caron's game blossomed. After an impressive freshman year, Caron emerged as a superstar in his sophomore season, averaging 20.3 points a game and earning recognition as a co–Big East Player of the Year, leading the Huskies to the regional finals of the 2002 NCAA Tournament. Caron scored a whopping thirty-two points in a loss against Maryland, the eventual champions.

Caron declared himself eligible for the NBA Draft that year and was selected by the Miami Heat with the tenth overall pick. He continued to turn heads at the professional level. In his first season in the NBA, Caron averaged an impressive 15.4 points and 5.1 rebounds per game on his way to making the All-Rookie First Team.

Throughout his successful career, Caron has been a leading player for several teams, as well as a two-time NBA All-Star. Caron also was a key member of the 2011 Dallas Mavericks, winning a championship ring with the team that year.

When his career is over, though, Caron likely will be remembered for his influence on stars throughout the league. Many of these players admire Caron for all that he overcame, even more so than for his scoring and rebounding abilities.

"Caron Butler was the big brother I needed," according to Dwyane Wade, who played with Caron during Wade's rookie year on the Miami Heat and described him a "true mentor."

Dwyane has said that Caron helped teach that excelling at sports is not as important as excelling in life, something Wade called "the big picture."

Several teams have traded for Caron in the hopes that his personality, toughness, and determination might rub off on teammates. In 2011, the Los Angeles Clippers were intent on building a winning squad and wanted to lure point guard Chris Paul to the team to join their superstar forward Blake Griffin and other young talent. Before they could trade for Paul, though, the team signed Caron to a three-year, twenty-four-million-dollar contract, a sum considered above market at the time.

The team knew that Butler provided the credibility, leadership, guts, and competitiveness a winning team needed. The signing also sent a signal to Paul that the Clippers were serious about winning. Indeed, shortly after the signing, Paul agreed to a trade to come to Los Angeles.

In 2014, the Oklahoma City Thunder also jumped at the chance to trade for Caron. "The thing that we really like about him is he's resilient," Thunder general manager Sam Presti said at the time. "He's a grinder and he's tough-minded, and he's a guy that's got great bounce-back. Those are things that we value."

Today, Caron owns six Burger King franchises across the country—a far cry from the days when he was tasked with cleaning up fry grease at the Racine restaurant after his stint in prison. He's also taken business-management courses at Duke University. But Caron never forgot his old neighborhood. Over the years, he's donated over a thousand coats and bicycles to children in Racine, and he regularly conducts basketball clinics in the city.

In 2007, Caron returned to Racine for Caron Butler Day, when he was honored for all his accomplishments. That day, Caron broke down and cried when he was given an award by the city. Caron even visited the White House in 2015 with Lieutenant Richard Geller—the officer who decided not to arrest him years earlier—to meet Vice President Joe Biden and Attorney General Loretta Lynch and discuss ways of improving communication between youth and police. It was a clear sign of how far he's come from the streets of Racine.

In recent years, Caron has become vocal about sharing lessons from his tumultuous life.

"There might be a kid out there who has been through some bad things, and maybe seeing me, someone who has been through the things I've been through, will help them," Caron told the *Washington Post*. "I don't necessarily mean playing in the NBA. It can be school. It can be music. It might be helping other people. There are so many better things that you can do with your life. We all go through some difficult things, but once those things happen, the question is, How are you going to respond?"

Caron's response is clear: Ignore negative influences and do whatever it takes to live a productive and upstanding life.

JACQUES DEMERS

F ew can match the coaching career of Jacques Demers. Over twenty years behind the benches of hockey franchises, including the Detroit Red Wings, St. Louis Blues, and Quebec Nordiques, his teams earned ten National Hockey League Play-off appearances. Jacques also coached the Montreal Canadiens to victory in the 1993 Stanley Cup Championship. To this day, he is the only person in NHL history to be named Coach of the Year two years in a row.

After retiring from coaching, Jacques's career in the world of hockey continued in a different capacity, as he took on the role of a color commentator for NHL television broadcasts. In 2009, Jacques shifted gears and left hockey behind to pursue a new calling, joining the Canadian parliament as a senator.

Throughout his coaching career, Jacques had been

known as a popular and intelligent presence behind the bench and in the locker room. But Jacques hid a humiliating secret throughout his life, one he desperately hoped no one would find out. He could barely read or write. It wasn't until he turned sixty-one years old that Jacques revealed the truth to the public.

As a young boy, Jacques was badly abused by his alcoholic father. He tried his best in school, but his life was filled with so much anxiety and chaos that he often couldn't focus on his studies. Reading and writing came naturally to others, but for Jacques the process of learning such skills was an embarrassing struggle.

"Kids teased me," he says. "They thought I was dumb and stupid."

Later, when he became a coach, Jacques lived in constant fear someone might discover his secret. Who would hire a coach who couldn't read a scouting report or write words of encouragement on a locker room chalkboard?

Jacques was so worried his secret might get out that he didn't even share it with his own family, in case they slipped up and told friends or others. He decided he'd have to go through life praying no one found out. The pressure to guard the secret was intense; Jacques couldn't let his guard down even for a moment.

"I was just afraid," he says. "I had to keep my big secret."

From an early age, Jacques faced serious challenges. Growing up in Montreal's Côte-des-Neiges neighborhood, Jacque's family was poor. His father, Emile, worked as a janitor for local buildings and the family received a free apartment in exchange for his labor. But his father was such a heavy drinker that he rarely showed up for work or did an adequate job when he actually made it in for the day.

To keep the family from being evicted, ten-year-old Jacques and his two older sisters began helping their father out. Sometimes, Jacques woke in the middle of the night to put coals in a furnace for twenty or more apartments, keeping them warm in the freezing Canadian winter. He and his sisters did other demanding work when their father was drunk or not around.

"It got to the point where we had to take over as janitors, picking up garbage" and doing other menial labor because their father was drunk or not around, Jacques says.

The help the Demers kids gave their father usually wasn't enough, though. Eventually, he'd lose his job and the family would be kicked out. Their prospects improved when a new building needed a janitor and the family moved their stuff into a new apartment. But the alcohol would flow, Jacques's father would get fired, and the Demers family would be out in the cold once again.

"It got to the point where it wasn't a big deal to have to move on all the time," he says.

As tension in the household built, Emile lashed out at Jacques and his sisters, usually for no good reason. If Jacques made a mistake around the house, Emile would scream at Jacques or hit him. Jacques also got slapped when he *didn't* misbehave or make a mistake.

The insults hurt most of all. "You're dumb and stupid," Jacques father would say before smacking him across the head. "You'll never amount to anything."

Jacques took the abuse without putting up much of a fight.

"You don't touch your dad," he explains. "But it had a huge effect on my self-confidence."

One day, Emile got really angry. He told his son to go home and wait for him. Jacques sat for hours, barely moving, scared his father would catch him away from the chair. Jacques was afraid to even go to the bathroom. He sat around waiting for so long he eventually wet his pants.

Jacque's mother, Mignonne, couldn't bear to watch

her son be treated so cruelly. Emile was a big man, weighing 200 pounds. Mignonne was tiny, barely over one hundred pounds. But when Emile called Jacques "worthless" his mother often stepped in, telling Emile to stop.

"You're a brave young boy," she told Jacques, building his confidence after another beating.

That made Jacques's father even angrier. Jacques's mom may have been slight of stature, but that didn't prevent Emile from smacking her around. One time, Emile slapped Mignonne so hard he split her eyebrow. As blood gushed, Jacques watched in silence, unable to help.

"My mom defended me and she paid the price," Jacques says.

In the 1950s, divorce was rare in French Canada, so Mignonne endured regular beatings, Jacques suffering along with his mother. She wouldn't go to the doctor and sometimes avoided leaving her home, to avoid questions from neighbors about the welts on her face. When Jacques's family did leave the house, they were often met with stares.

"The neighbors would look at us funny," Jacques says. "We would lie and say everything was fine."

At one point during middle school, Jacques's family

moved to an affluent suburb of Montreal called Out-remont when his father got a job. Jacques, who tried to be cheerful despite his troubles at home, began attending a French-speaking school, hoping the change of scenery might bring him better fortune.

When he got to school, though, Jacques realized he didn't look anything like his classmates. They all wore new, expensive clothing; Jacque's discount-store clothing stood out. Bullies targeted him, teasing him for his wardrobe and appearance.

"They made fun of me because I didn't have the same clothing," Jacques says. "I took it to heart."

Many young people dealing with upheaval turn bitter, lashing out at teachers or friends. Jacques had his share of anger. But he tried to focus on the positives in his life, smiling through the pain and ignoring his father and the bullies as best he could.

"I had a blockage when it came to my dad: I just didn't listen to him [when he screamed]," Jacques recalls. "I just wanted to be a happy kid."

To find some peace, Jacques sometimes spent the night with his grandmother and aunt. They gave him love and nourishment, though he never shared details of what was going on at home.

Jacques got an after-school job delivering groceries

to local customers, including some who spoke Yiddish, and the owner of a local grocery, Morris Wolf, took a liking to the boy and invited him to spend time with his family. Jacques became a regular in the Wolf home, playing with his four boys, vowing to build a loving family of his own one day.

"In some ways, I was raised by that Jewish family," Jacques says. "They took care of me and were so family oriented; I wanted to be like them."

By then, Jacques had discovered the hockey rink. There it was possible—even encouraged—to take aggressions out on opponents through physical play, a useful outlet for Jacques. Friendly off the ice, he surprised himself by throwing hard checks and starting fights once the puck was dropped.

Jacques wasn't a thug or an enforcer, just a tough player with an edge.

"I was an angry young boy inside, but it only showed up in sports," he says. "Someone would do something to me in a game, and I wanted to fight. That was my way of dealing with stuff. I needed to get it out."

Jacques wasn't the most talented player on the rink, and it didn't seem likely he'd ever play professionally. But he seemed a born leader who gained the respect of teammates and usually was named captain of his team.

At home, the violence continued. Jacques watched as his mother's forehead was bloodied on a regular basis. He and his sisters rarely had a full night's sleep. If they weren't being emotionally or physically hurt, they would lie awake, worried that a new round of fury was a beer away.

"Back then, you never reported abuse like that; you kept your mouth shut," Jacques says.

At night, Jacques often hid under a blanket, crying and worrying about his mother while trying to shield himself from the turmoil. After a night full of violent disturbances, Jacques was exhausted at school. He couldn't manage to concentrate. He continued to keep his family's secrets so teachers had no idea what was going on at home.

"They just saw my failures at school," he says. "I would go to class, but I wasn't really there."

Full of anxiety and unable to pay attention in class, Jacques continued to struggle with reading and writing.

Why can't I get it like other kids? Jacques kept asking himself.

"I couldn't pick it up," Jacques says. "You start questioning yourself. It really bothered me."

Jacques wanted to read and write like his class-mates. He also knew if he brought home a bad report card his father would be furious. Somehow, he had to find a way to get decent grades. Eventually, Jacques developed ways of convincing teachers he was keeping up. He also got help from his sisters and friends, who pitched in to help him with his homework.

"It was a struggle, but I got by," he says. "I never cheated, but my friends helped a lot. . . . I knew if I didn't have a decent report card, I'd get it at home."

Jacques barely managed to get by at school, but circumstances at home took an even darker turn. When Jacques turned thirteen, the family found out that his mother had leukemia. She had tremen-dous courage and tried her best to fight the cancer. But her sickness added further strain to the family, and Emile's drinking continued, making school even more challenging.

"I was tired and distracted and worried about Mom," Jacques says.

As he began eighth grade, Jacques was functionally illiterate, or unable to read or write more than very sim-ple sentences. There were so many aspects of Jacques's life that contributed to his struggles: his father's abuse, the family's financial troubles, his lack of sleep, and the constant burden of helping out around the home. Above all else, Jacques's mother's health was the most upsetting factor. She was his only protector and he loved her so much. But his mother's cancer was getting worse, and he worried she wouldn't make it.

As the cancer progressed and Mignonne weakened, Emile stopped hitting his wife, a welcome relief for Jacques and his sisters.

"At that point, she was so frail and weak," Jacques says. "God did her a favor" by making her so sick.

As Jacques grew bigger, his father stopped beating him as well, perhaps afraid Jacques might return the blows.

One day, Jacques and his sisters went to the hospital. It was clear their mother didn't have much time left. She wanted Jacques to make her a promise.

"Take care of your sisters, and don't be like your dad," she asked Jacques.

He vowed to keep the promise the rest of his life. "I just didn't want to disappoint her."

For Jacques, it was a crushing experience. He had lost the one person in his life who loved and protected him.

· · ·

Jacques dropped out of school before finishing eighth grade to help support his family.

He was just sixteen. But he was determined to make his mother proud.

"I had to do something with my life, but I just didn't know what it was," he says.

Jacques continued to have a relationship with his father, hoping he'd finally show him some love. In 1964, four years after his mother's death, Jacques drove with his father to Jacques's sister's wedding. On the way home, Jacques's father lurched forward, his head hitting the dashboard. He leaned toward Jacques, dying of a heart attack.

"I cried," Jacques told the *Montrealer* in 2006. "Can you believe that? After all he had done—I cried. I just wanted my father to love me."

Without his parents around, Jacques was confused and worried about his future.

"I was twenty years old and alone," he says. "I had to survive."

Jacques had played Junior B Hockey and loved the sport, modeling his game after Henri Richard, the Canadiens center who won a record eleven Stanley Cups but usually was overshadowed by his more famous brother, Canadiens Hall of Famer Maurice "The Rocket" Richard.

"He wasn't a big guy, and it was tough for him to compete with his brother," Jacques says of Henri. "But he always gave his best."

Jacques never reached the highest level of Junior Hockey. At five feet eleven and 175 pounds, he wasn't big or strong enough. He wasn't quite skilled enough, either. Jacques was more of a leader than a scorer, serving as a constant source of support and guidance for his teammates. "I wouldn't yell [at my teammates]," Jacques says, "but I'd say, 'Let's play harder, guys.'"

But Jacques's strong leadership skills weren't enough to earn him a spot playing for a professional hockey team, and he still needed to figure out his plan for the future. Since Jacques had dropped out of school and knew he wasn't going to make the NHL, he started looking for a job. Eventually, he found one driving a Coca-Cola truck.

Jacques still had a passion for hockey. Sometimes, he managed to talk his way into Montreal Canadiens practices to watch and learn. Jacques's brother-in-law was involved with the local Junior Ice Hockey program and needed coaching help. One day, he asked Jacques to lend a hand.

Jacques began coaching fourteen- and fifteen-year-olds. Before long, he was leading older kids to championships. He was having a blast and thought he might be able to get a job coaching at a higher Junior Hockey league in Quebec or elsewhere, so he asked his bosses at Coca-Cola to hold his job for him while he tried coaching.

Coca-Cola turned him down. Jacques gave up on the idea of earning his living by coaching hockey, worried he'd be left without a job if he couldn't find a position or if his team played poorly. Memories of the brutal poverty of his youth forced him to give up on his dream.

"I thought, if I wasn't successful, where would I get work?" he says.

Jacques decided to make the best of his situation by continuing to coach the teenagers in the Junior B League.

"I always thought, if you sit in your chair at home . . . complaining, nothing good will happen," Jacques says. "If you're out there and work hard, something good could happen."

He had good instincts. One day, Jacques Beauchamp,

a well-known sports writer for *Le Journal de Montréal*, noticed how effective Jacques was behind the bench and wrote a flattering profile in his paper. The young coach had a touch with his players and was a remarkable motivator, Beauchamp wrote, and his teams always seemed to win.

Beauchamp reached out to Marcel Pronovost, a former NHL Hall of Famer who was coaching the Chicago Cougars in a new pro hockey league called the World Hockey Association. The league needed assistant coaches, and Beauchamp recommended Jacques for a position. This time, Jacques quit his job at Coke and grabbed the opportunity to coach professionally. He knew there was big risk getting into coaching, but he loved it so much he was willing to take the chance.

At the beginning of the 1975 season, Jacques moved to the Unites States to lead the Indianapolis Racers. He had never coached professionally and he was just twenty-eight years old. Some of his players were older than he was, and it wasn't clear whether or not he'd be able to command their respect.

From opening night, however, it was obvious there was something special about Jacques and his coaching. He possessed a vast knowledge of the game and was adept at devising strategies. More important, Jacques loved his players and showed them more support than they ever had received, giving them confidence to perform at a high level.

"You're my players; I'm going to listen to *you*," Jacques told his team.

It was as if he had learned from his father what *not* to do when dealing with those around him. Unlike his father, Jacques didn't berate his players, choosing to look out for their well-being instead. Players sought Jacques out to share details of their lives, not just to talk hockey.

"My style was to create a family," Jacques says.

In an unintended way, his father had helped Jacques develop a unique and successful approach to coaching.

"As a young boy, I was always looking for love; I wanted to be told I was a good guy," Jacques says. "So when I became a coach, I became fatherly. My dad wouldn't listen to me, but I decided to be supportive of my players, treat them with respect, and listen to them."

In Indianapolis, Jacques's team won the Eastern Division Championship. Following his initial success, he accepted two more coaching jobs in the WHA and continued to be a popular presence behind the bench. Players gave their all for Jacques, and he continued to help them win.

Jacques got a lucky break in 1983 when he was hired to coach the National Hockey League's St. Louis Blues. There was just one problem: Jacques still didn't know how to read or write. His deficiencies hadn't tripped him up yet, but now Jacques had more to lose. He was scared to tell anyone or let his secret become public knowledge, worried he'd lose his job and his new life as a professional hockey coach and have to go back to driving a truck.

Jacques vowed to keep his secret from his players and his bosses, going to great lengths to ensure that information stayed hidden. Before games, Jacques had his assistants read him scouting reports, which he would memorize. His assistants compiled rosters, summed up reports, and did other writing-related tasks that were usually expected of coaches. On road trips, Jacques brought piles of newspapers and magazines and pretended to read them while trying to teach himself a word or two.

At restaurants, Jacques usually ordered the filet mignon or one of the specials the waiter had offered after pretending to read the menu. When there was something that needed to be read, Jacques asked others to help, saying his English wasn't very good. Later in his career, when he coached in French-speaking Quebec

City, Jacques said he had spent so much time in the United States that his French was rusty. Others would read him newspaper articles and pay his bills. To stay in touch with daily events, Jacques became an avid viewer of CNN.

Jacques developed more elaborate tricks. He began wearing glasses, for example, though he didn't need them. If he was put on the spot and asked to read or write something, Jacques would pat his chest, look for his glasses, and then shrug.

"Ooh, I misplaced my glasses," he would respond, even though the glasses usually were buried deep in his pocket.

Jacques was great with numbers and figures, emphasizing statistics in his conversations with players and the media. And he impressed audiences with his upbeat, captivating speeches, which he recited by heart.

"I speak well and I have good judgment; that part I did well," he says. "I got up every morning with a lot of energy and a smile on my face. I had to offset what I didn't have. . . . I owe that to my mom, she was always nice to people and smiling."

Friends had no idea Jacques had trouble reading and writing. When he went to his friend Sam Eltes's automobile dealership in Montreal to buy a new car, Jacques would ask Sam to fill in the proper amount on the check, Eltes recalls.

"If I came out and admitted things, I'd be made fun of and I wouldn't get another job in the NHL, that was my fear," he says. "I had four kids to feed and I was getting older. I didn't want to lose my job."

Jacques didn't even tell the secret to the woman he would marry, Debbie Anderson.

"I was afraid she'd leave me," he says. "I had been divorced twice and I wasn't sure I could be in a marriage. I wasn't brought up with love. I didn't know how to do it."

In 1984, while coaching the Blues, Jacques returned from a road trip and saw a pile of bills that Debbie had neglected to pay.

"Why didn't you pay the bills?" he asked.

"I'm not your secretary," Debbie responded.

Jacques turned unusually angry, tossing the bills on the kitchen floor.

"Well, they won't be paid, then," Jacques said, overcome with emotion, "because I can't write those checks."

He broke down in tears, confessing to Debbie that he was illiterate.

"I felt desperation," he says. "She was a stenographer and very smart; I knew she was going to catch me."

Jacques still wasn't willing to open up to his children from his earlier marriages, worried they might tell their spouses and the secret might leak out to the public. Jacques shared his weakness with just one other person, reporter Mario Leclerc, who inadvertently discovered that Jacques couldn't read or write. He swore Leclerc to secrecy.

"It wasn't meant to fool anyone, just to protect myself," Jacques says.

His mother had thought she needed to keep quiet about the abuse she had received. Jacques took the same approach, convinced there was no one he could trust with his own secret.

On the ice, Jacques's outgoing approach was effective. Jacques took the Detroit Red Wings from last place to the play-offs in the 1986–1987 season and followed that up with another strong performance the next year, winning the coach of the year title in back-to-back seasons. In 1993, Jacques was celebrated by fans all across Canada after coaching the Canadiens to a Stanley Cup Championship.

"He was always trying to create a family, and he was successful at it," said Guy Carbonneau, a former

Canadiens captain under Demers, during an interview on ESPN. "He was always up and upbeat. Always trying to turn a bad situation into a good situation."

Hiding a huge secret caused anxiety, though, and anger sometimes emerged. A few times, Jacques got so upset at opposing coaches that he tried to attack them during big games, a sign that he was struggling to hide something important just below the surface.

In 1998, Jacques's secret was suddenly at risk of being revealed. While trying to turn around a Tampa Bay Lightning team that had been awful for years, Jacques was called into the office of owner Art Williams. Williams had just fired Phil Esposito, the team's legendary general manager. Now he had a surprising request for Jacques.

"I want you to be my general manager *and* my coach," Williams said.

Jacques was in a quandary. He felt honored to receive the offer, but he also was scared. A general manager runs an organization, negotiates contracts, and evaluates talent. Jacques knew his inability to read or write would be a huge handicap. He also realized there was a good chance someone would discover his weakness.

But Jacques knew if he turned down the offer or

admitted he was functionally illiterate, he'd be fired on the spot. Williams had made it clear to the media that Jacques's job was on thin ice.

"Jacques is not safe by any means," Williams told reporters. "He's not safe at all."

Jacques accepted the job, but he made a request of Williams.

"I'll take the job, but I need to hire someone to help me," Jacques said.

Williams agreed, figuring Jacques was simply concerned that being a coach and general manger would be too burdensome. Jacques ended up hiring others to work on contracts and assume other duties he couldn't perform on his own. That year, the Lightning drafted a young player named Vincent Lecavalier, who became a huge star. The pick marked a great start to Jacques's tenure.

It wasn't enough, though. Tampa went 34–109 over two seasons and missed the play-offs each year. Hiding a secret was too much of a burden for Jacques, as was the challenge of turning around a team with little talent. When Williams sold the team in 1999, Jacques was fired, and his coaching career ended.

•   •   •

After retiring from coaching, Jacques started working as a television analyst for the Montreal Canadiens. It was a prestigious position and Jacques was thrilled to get the offer, but without coaching to distract him, he grew angrier. Debbie urged Jacques to see a psychiatrist and work on his mental health issues. After months of pleading, Jacques finally consented. But he insisted on going through the back door of the doctor's office for his early appointments, rather than the usual front entrance.

"I was still ashamed and worried someone would see me," he says.

Over time, Jacques came to grips with his difficult childhood. He also discovered he had learning issues but wasn't "dumb," which came as a relief. Medications helped him control his anxiety, and he became calmer.

By 2003, Jacques was ready to open up about his illiteracy, hoping his story might give encouragement to young people going through their own challenges. Together with Mario Leclerc, Jacques wrote a French-language book called *Jacques Demers: En Toutes Lettres*, which described his unhappy childhood and his battle to hide his reading and writing difficulties.

The night before the book was published in 2005,

Jacques was gripped with fear about how his children would react to the disclosure that their father was functionally illiterate. Jacques forced himself to pick up the phone to call his kids, holding his breath as he anticipated what they would say about the secret he'd spent a lifetime hiding.

Their reaction came as a shock to Jacques.

"Dad, why didn't you tell us before?" said his youngest son, Jason, who was twenty-four years old at the time.

"I was afraid you'd be ashamed of me," Jacques replied.

"Dad, we love you," Jason said through tears. "And we're proud of you."

Jacques's problems weren't as unique as he thought. The most recent study by the National Center for Education Statistics showed that thirty-two million American adults, or 14 percent of the population, has "below basic" reading and writing skills. Many of these people live in poverty.

Adults from all walks of life reached out to Jacques, including businessmen and older hockey players, to share their own reading and writing challenges.

"I've been hiding, too," a salesman told Jacques one day. "I don't want my boss to find out."

"You should share it; you're suffering inside," Jacques told him. "I wish I had opened up earlier."

Jacques began traveling across the United States and Canada, speaking to children, adults, and prisoners, encouraging brave individuals to confess their own secrets and sharing advice about how to deal with life's difficulties.

"Don't give up," he tells them. "Everything was a fight for me."

Don't lose faith in yourself, Jacques says, and don't lose hope.

"You can say a life started very badly, but maybe it will end very well," he says.

Today, Jacques is a senator in the Canadian parliament. The seventy-one-year-old is still working on his reading and writing, learning a few words a day. He doesn't yet have confidence in his writing. But after years of living with a deep sense of shame, fear, and embarrassment, Jacques recently reached an important goal: He managed to read his own book.

AFTERWORD

One fall day in late 2014, my son Eli came up with a wonderful idea. Many athletes playing different sports have overcome tremendous obstacles that at one time seemed insurmountable. Why don't we write a book to tell their amazing stories? As a newspaper reporter with a lifelong interest in how individuals achieve greatness, I was intrigued. When Eli's brother, Gabriel, got excited about the project, we were on our way, tracking down players to learn the incredible details of their life stories.

We each had our own unique reasons to write this book. Fourteen-year-old Eli is a sports nut, autograph hound and star athlete. He wanted to discover the best sports stories and share them with young people his age. Eli also was born with a difference and was eager to hear how stars dealt with their own challenges. Gabriel, a seventeen-year-old bookworm and stalwart defender on the soccer pitch, was in search of gripping life stories to entertain teenagers and older readers. For my part, I was sure the stars' life lessons would be inspirational and instructive to young kids and teens dealing with their own misfortune and difficulties. I also was convinced parents would find the stories as affecting and uplifting as I did.

We began speaking with stars from many professional sports—basketball, baseball, soccer, tennis, and hockey. The athletes told moving and compelling tales with enough twists and turns to fill the big screen of any movie theater.

The players featured in the book seemed especially eager to share their life lessons with Eli and Gabriel, a sign of their hope that their stories might help young people around the world. The stars clearly wanted to spare readers some of the pain they had endured in their youth.

The athletes dealt with a diverse array of obstacles, including physical differences, childhoods filled with drugs and violence, hardship, and abuse. The surprise was to discover how each superstar views his or her unique challenge as a gift. Stephen Curry spoke of how early failures helped him become one of the NBA's greatest shooters. Tim Howard said there was a "beautiful flip side" to the Tourette syndrome that affects him. Shane Battier emphasized how being different "is what makes life fun." And Serge Ibaka said the tough times he overcame demonstrated that no matter how bleak life seems, better times might be ahead.

Everyone, young and old, has a difference, something that sets her or him apart in a way that might seem like a weakness. And many people have dealt with imposing setbacks. But sometimes challenges can be opportunities, rather than merely obstacles. The athletes in this book are a testament to the idea that with the right guidance, mind-set, and dedication, any young person can overcome adversity and excel in the world.

ACKNOWLEDGMENTS

We'd like to thank Stephen Curry, Tim Howard, Serge Ibaka, R.A. Dickey, Jim Abbott, Venus Williams, Shane Battier, and Jacques Demers, all of whom generously took time to share thoughts, stories, and lessons from their youth.

We were lucky to have a great group of supporters rooting us on as we worked on this project. Mark Gerson provided invaluable introductions to key stars. John Prato lent his own assistance. Susie, Hannah, Rebecca, Nathan, and Liora Nussbaum cheered us from day one; we appreciate you guys so much. Adam Brauer, Harold Simansky, and Alex Engel were true fans of the effort, while Howard Morris and Roberto Krutiansky kindly read sections of the manuscript. Jeremiah Klapper shared smart tips of players worthy of featuring.

Last but not least, Michelle Zuckerman couldn't have been more supportive and encouraging. You're the best mother and wife anyone could ask for. We love you.

BIBLIOGRAPHY

Stephen Curry

1) *E:60*, ESPN, April 24, 2014

2) Ben Cohen, "Stephen Curry's Science of Sweet Shooting," *The Wall Street Journal*, December 17, 2014

3) Stu Woo, "Two Things Stephen Curry Does Better Than You," *The Wall Street Journal*, May 7, 2013

Tim Howard

1) Tim Howard with Ali Benjamin, *The Keeper: The Unguarded Story of Tim Howard (Young Readers' Edition)*, New York: HarperCollins Publishers, 2014

LeBron James

1) Tom Friend, "Next: LeBron James," *ESPN The Magazine*, December 10, 2002

2) LeBron James and Buzz Bissinger, *Shooting Stars*, New York: Penguin Press, 2009

3) Chris Tomasson, "LeBron James Credits Peewee Coach for Lefty Layup," *Florida & Sun Sports*, May 23, 2013

4) Eli Saslow, "Lost Stories of LeBron, Part 1," *ESPN The Magazine*, October 19, 2013

5) Dan Robson, "I Promise to Never Forget Where I Came From," Sportsnet, September 29, 2014

R.A. Dickey

1) R.A. Dickey and Wayne Coffey, *Wherever I Wind Up: My Quest for Truth, Authenticity, and the Perfect Knuckleball*, New York: Blue Rider Press, 2012

Caron Butler

1) Dan Steinberg, "Caron Butler Takes Readers Inside a Life Filled with Guns, Guts and Grit," *Washington Post*, September 22, 2015

2) Darnell Mayberry, "Caron Butler's Remarkable Story Will Now Include an OKC Chapter," NewsOK, March 3, 2014

3) Michael Lee, "The Great Escape," *Washington Post*, February 17, 2008

4) Ivan Carter, "Butler's Life Has Come Full Circle," *Washington Post*, September 9, 2005

5) *The Story of Caron Butler*, Fox Sports Live, February 16, 2014

6) *Caron Butler on the Hustle*, Vice Sports, September 3, 2014

Althea Gibson

1) Althea Gibson, *I Always Wanted To Be Somebody*, New York: The Curtis Publishing Company, 1958

2) Frances Clayton Gray and Yanick Rice Lamb, *Born to Win: The Authorized Biography of Althea Gibson*, Hoboken, New Jersey: John Wiley & Sons, Inc., 2004

3) "Althea Gibson wins Wimbledon," History.com, http://www.history.com/this-day-in-history/althea-gibson-wins-wimbledon

Serge Ibaka

1) Darnell Mayberry, "Coming to America: How Serge Ibaka Went from the Congo to the NBA," NewsOK, April 13, 2010

2) *Son of the Congo*, Grantland, June 30, 2015

Jim Abbott

1) Jim Abbott and Tim Brown, *Imperfect: An Improbable Life*, New York: Ballantine Books, 2012

2) Mike Foss, "20 Years Ago Today, A One-Handed Yankee Pitched a No-Hitter," *USA Today*, September 4, 2013

Shane Battier

1) Tom Haberstroh, "Shane Battier's Biggest Pet Peeve," ESPN, January 5, 2012

2) Michael Lewis, "The No-Stats All-Star," *New York Times Magazine*, February 13, 2009

Jacques Demers

1) Mitch Albom, "The Painful Secret That Millions Hide: I Cannot Read," *Parade Magazine*, February 12, 2006

2) Hillel Kuttler, "Coach Jacques Demers Hoping to Add Another Maccabiah Gold to Stanley Cup, Victory Over Illiteracy," *Jewish Telegraphic Agency*, July 16, 2013

3) "Jacques Demers from A to Z," *The Montrealer*, April 1, www.themontrealeronline.com/2006/04/jacques-demers-from-a-to-z/

4) Clifford Krauss, "His Life in Hockey, From A to . . . Well, Never Past A," *New York Times*, November 12, 2005

5) Scott Burnside, "Demers' Secret Struggle with Pain, Shame of Illiteracy," ESPN, November 7, 2005

Dwyane Wade

1) Dwyane Wade, *A Father First: How My Life Became Bigger than Basketball*, New York: William Morrow, 2012

2) Associated Press, "Wade Buys Mom a Church After She Completes Turnaround," May 18, 2008, http://sports.espn.go.com/nba/news/story?id=3402358

3) Michelle Wilson, "Jolinda Wade: 'He Can Bring You Through,'" *The 700 Club*, CBN TV, February 18, 2013

4) *E:60*, Dwyane Wade Interview, ESPN, March 5, 2011

INDEX